Mindful Mixology

Mindful Mixology

**A Comprehensive Guide to
No- and Low-Alcohol Cocktails**

Derek Brown
Photographs by Nole Garey

RIZZOLI
NEW YORK

New York · Paris · London · Milan

To the reason I prefer clear-headed mornings to besotted nights, my son.

Table of Contents

Foreword
Julia Bainbridge

When Roxana B. Doran published her drinks book *Prohibition Punches* in 1930, a reporter for *The Sunday Star* wrote that Doran "initiated the kick-less cocktail movement." Apparently these "innocuous recipes" were being "taken up by the social elite of the national capitol." Gooseberry Punch—it called for fresh gooseberry juice, which is something to which I guess said social elite had access—was among these "innocent appetizers without alcohol."

I know all of this because Derek Brown texted me a link to a vintage cocktail book website at 12:42 a.m. a couple of years ago. That link was followed by screenshots of various archival materials on related subjects, enough to classify the collection as a veritable stream—nay, river—of research findings.

This is what you get when you're friends with Derek and share a particular interest. He is a seeker; he is perhaps a bit obsessive; he is most definitely a geek. (He led home mixologists, amateur historians, and anthropologists in a four-part lecture series tracing the life of the American cocktail from its birth up to today for *Atlas Obscura*, okay?) But perhaps Derek's most endearing quality is his enthusiasm. Do you follow him on Twitter (@ideasimprove)? Then you might have seen the à la minute recipes he designed for his sheltering-in-place followers based on whatever ingredients they had on hand during the coronavirus pandemic. Or his soliloquy about cocktails as liquid cultural artifacts and mirrors to humanity on National Cocktail Day last March. He loves this stuff.

Doran, by the way, was the wife of James M. Doran, the United States Commissioner of Prohibition. Her book came out three years before the unpopular 18th Amendment, which had banned the consumption of alcohol, was repealed. So, while there's something to be learned from her recipes—and you can trust that Derek has studied them—this book comes at a time when choosing a low- or no-alcohol cocktail is just that: a choice.

Derek's own choices have changed over the years, and he now consumes much less alcohol than he used to. Mix his natural curiosity, tenacity, and generosity with an immersion in the world of nonalcoholic drinks, and you have mindful mixology. While many champion alcohol-free cocktails by making vague references to "sophisticated" flavors that are more "complex" than sugary, one-note sodas, Derek pushes himself to better understand and articulate the details. What makes for an "adult" beverage? What even is a cocktail, really? What is it that we love about it? How can we offer those experiences without alcohol? With my own compendium of alcohol-free recipes called *Good Drinks*, I essentially drew a circle around today's alcohol-free landscape. Derek, with his decades of experience as a professional bartender, offers the tenets of building these cocktails, a way to codify them, and all the technical particulars.

And, yes, enthusiasm.

I did eventually respond to Derek's late-night text—at a reasonable hour—a couple of days later. "I thumbed through a digital copy of this book," I wrote. "Phi Tau Freeze, contributed by Phi Kappa Tau Fraternity: 'To 1 gallon ginger ale add 1 quart of pure orange juice. Just before serving add 2 quarts of orange sherbet. Beat into frappé.' Alcohol-free orange frosé? I'll take it." His response: "!!" And then I responded, and he responded, and I responded again, and it went on and on like that until, well, now. I hope this conversation between us—and between all of you—never ends.

Introduction
Mindful Drinking

The first thing people would say, when I told them I'm writing a book on low- and no-alcohol cocktails, is: "Can I add booze to the recipes?" It was a joke, of course. But, much to the surprise of the interlocutor, I would confess, "yes." There was an expectation that because I make low- and no-alcohol drinks I'm a teetotaler, and I would scoff at the thought of adding the hard stuff. But I didn't. I wouldn't. I'm a bartender by trade, I write on cocktails and spirits, and own one of America's top cocktail bars, Columbia Room. I'm not averse to alcohol, I'm immersed in it.

That immersion has brought me some joy and recognition for my craft, but it's also brought a fair amount of pain and suffering. Especially when I had to wake up and take care of both my son and hungover self. I'd heat up a bottle and grab the Pedialyte (the Pedialyte was for me, bottle for him), pray that my son would nap—often, to no avail—and begin the grueling punishment of watching a child with the hangover-magnifying trifecta of baby giggles, tears, and refuse. It seems obvious in retrospect, but hangovers and the duties of parenthood are not entirely compatible.

But baby duty wasn't the only thing that contributed to my pain and suffering. The lifestyle of a young bartender and bar owner, awash with all the trappings of rock stars except worldwide fame, had led past late nights into early mornings and—too many drinks in—to make decisions I would come to regret. Alcohol was an excuse for me to behave badly and to ignore my mental health issues, which only compounded my behavior. Being drunk, I could live in a fantasy world and didn't have to consider the repercussions of my actions or the low-idling engine of anxiety anymore. I was living in that drunken moment, free of concern, even if that moment was wobbly, blurry, and soon forgotten. My relationships were strained. My health was suboptimal. My pocketbook was tight. I wasn't at my best, or even close. I'd convinced myself it was a choice. It wasn't.

Once I added up the ledger of the good and bad from my relationship with alcohol, I realized it had cost me far too much (which is the subject of another book). It was time to ask myself a question: Why do I drink alcohol? I know why I serve alcohol: It's my job, and I love what I do. But why do I, a human being, drink alcohol? The answer was: for all the wrong reasons.

I took some time off, spent more clearheaded time with my son, sought help through therapy and medicine, and slowly integrated alcohol back into my life. I now drink maybe two alcoholic drinks a month and happily explore low or no-alcohol options. I take it easy. And I don't let my alcohol consumption be driven by compulsion. It's there, or it isn't. Either way, I'll live.

For me, this is mindful drinking.

Your reasons might be completely different. Maybe you've chosen to reduce your alcohol consumption for health reasons, piety, or you just don't like the way you feel after drinking. It doesn't matter. If you aren't drinking at all or aren't drinking a lot of alcohol, this book is for you.

Fortunately, there are others who feel the same way as we do. Over the last couple of years, we've seen groups celebrating mindful drinking, sober bars (without alcohol), and conferences pushing low- and no-alcohol options. It doesn't have to be all or nothing. You have options. And you can explore those options on your own terms.

What, then, is mindful mixology?

If mindful drinking is about weighing your options, then mindful mixology is an extension of that. You can learn the skills and recipes to enjoy a drink with little or no alcohol. In that way, I'm not asking you to sacrifice because you've curbed your drinking. I'm offering you a choice.

That choice is, drink alcohol, leave out the booze, go light, or mix it up. This isn't a binary choice, it's about a plethora of options, an embarrassment of options. You can have a drink with a friend that's sophisticated, dare I say even strong, and looks beautiful sans alcohol. You can have a drink, like I sometimes do, and make a second non-alcoholic cocktail. You can have a sessionable cocktail, a low-alcohol drink, or a few. This book is a book about options. But those options haven't always been apparent.

If you went to a bar before, the only options for mindful drinkers like us were soda or lemonade. Lovely drinks, really, but they make you feel a bit foolish when someone is having a sleek, crystalline Dry Martini. A Dry Martini looks shapely, bracingly cold, and oozes style. Coca-Cola, my favorite soda, just doesn't have the same cache: it's more picnics and kids' parties. Lemonade doesn't fare better. Both are delicious, but they don't do it for an adult gathering or at a bar. They feel like an afterthought. (And let's not start with the Shirley Temple.)

I don't want to be an afterthought. I want a sophisticated adult beverage, and I don't think it has to be boozy by default. But, while it doesn't have to be boozy, it does have to be good. And the blueprint for making great drinks already exists, we just have to look at mixology as a whole. Mindful mixology isn't about reinventing the wheel, only demonstrating its construction by other means.

Temperance Drinks

While mindful mixology has nothing to do with the temperance movement that drove Prohibition to be the ill-fated law of the land between 1919 and 1933 in the United States, I have found inspiration in temperance drinks. Take, for instance, the Old Time Temperance Cocktail. It was a hop and ginger long-drink from 1900. I made it into more of an Old Fashioned, letting the hops and ginger replace the bite of alcohol. Or Thompson's Spa Egg Phosphate, which was served at a sober bar, Thompson's, in the 1900s–it's a delightful, fluffy, sour.

I also found Temperance Drinks in the hallowed tomes of bartending such as Jerry Thomas' seminal *The Bon-Vivant's Guide, or How to Mix Drinks*, and David Embury's *The Fine Art of Mixing Drinks*. And in recipe guides from the early twentieth century, such as *On Uncle Sam's Water Wagon: 500 Recipes for Delicious Drinks, Which Can Be Made at Home*, by Helen Watkeys Moore.

I've always believed that the best drinks have likely already been discovered. Borrowing a piece of Solomonic wisdom: There is nothing new under the sun, even a Tequila Sunrise. There are many great recipes that I've changed only slightly, enhanced, or let be if they're perfect for how they are.

All in all, I'm happy to address questions about whether you can spike these drinks. You can, but you probably shouldn't. Because these drinks are plenty delicious without spiking them.

I've spent the last twenty years learning the ins and outs of mixology so you don't have to and I've spent the past five applying it mindfully. There is some wisdom in here but, more importantly, there is practical experience. Those are not always the same thing. But my experience, with a touch of wisdom, has led me to believe it's not about me. Mindful mixology is ultimately about you. Your headspace, your choice. Read the book in detail or pick a drink and start mixing. It's a Choose Your Own Adventure book in that way, but ultimately the reward for a journey completed is an excellent drink, with or without alcohol.

Mindful Cocktails

I didn't hit rock bottom. There wasn't an awful hangover and feeling that life needed to change. There was just this awareness over time that as an industry we needed to do something about the way we were drinking. Being a global ambassador for a large spirits company, I saw that we were losing too many people (to alcohol), my mentors, my friends.

I became a yoga teacher, a meditation teacher, and I asked myself: Do I belong in this industry. Maybe I've done my time? I was about to leave my role as a global ambassador, and decided to bring wellness, mindfulness, and cocktails together. I could combine wellness and hospitality through my company, La Maison Wellness. No one understood what I was doing, but I was on a journey to bring mindfulness to the glass.

Alcohol isn't what makes a cocktail special. It's the place, the atmosphere, the balance of the flavor, the person you're sharing the cocktail with—that whole experience. Food and drink have an incredible way of bringing us together. I want to inspire the industry and consumer how to drink better, celebrate everyday life, and live well. I want to be a force in changing the drinking culture and the conversation.

People will say, "I'm not drinking tonight," but they are. They're just not drinking alcohol. We've been educated on the place of alcohol in society, but we have the right to change the mold. To change the conversation. To grow and evolve, look into how we can celebrate our relationship with alcohol. And how we can celebrate in a more balanced way by discovering and adding mindful cocktails to our repertoire.

Camille Vidal
Founder, La Maison Wellness

Chapter One
Overview of
Mindful Mixology

You haven't read the word "mocktail" yet in this book for a reason: I don't like it. I realize mock this or that has a place in the vernacular—mock turtlenecks for instance—but I think it sounds silly and insulting when applied to cocktails. These drinks aren't fake cocktails or lesser cocktails—they're cocktails. I suppose that needs some clarification, but there's no other word that fits. I use non-alcoholic (NA) sometimes to acknowledge the drink has a corollary with booze—as in NA Getaway on page 111—but mocktails, spirit-free, zero proof all fall flat for me. It's a question of aesthetics, but then so are cocktails. I want to normalize drinking sophisticated adult drinks without alcohol and that means avoiding ridiculous or confusing names. So, to me, they're cocktails.

In my previous book, *Spirits, Sugar, Water, Bitters: How the Cocktail Conquered the World*, I answered the question, "What, then, is a Cocktail?" But there was one thing I left out. The cocktail I was discussing is alcoholic, made with spirits, sugar, water, and bitters. That definition comes from May 13, 1806, in *The Balance and Columbian Repository*, a paper from Hudson, New York. But the word cocktail indicating a beverage—not necessarily alcoholic—existed before that, appearing in the London newspaper *The Morning Post and Gazetteer*, March 20, 1798, discovered by cocktail historians Jared Brown and Anistatia Miller.

In the *The Morning Post And Gazetteer*, the writer uses political satire to discuss what then British prime minister, Mr. Pitt, ordered—"a 'cock-tail' (vulgarly called ginger)." Writer and historian David Wondrich has a theory about why the reference may not necessarily be to a drink with alcohol. He argues that the price is considerably lower than other drinks listed in the column with alcohol. (Anistatia Miller contends that the price is part of the joke.)

Wondrich's theory makes sense (though I'd be curious to see more of what Miller has to say). Before the word cocktail was a beverage, it was used in another context altogether, with ginger but no alcohol. It came from an unlikely place, or at least a place you wouldn't usually go looking for cocktails: a horse's rear. Racehorse owners would show their horses to prospective buyers with ginger shoved up the rectum, also called figging or feaguing, to increase the horse's sale value. It would then cause the horse to cock its tail and appear more lively (anyone would be lively under such circumstances). Wondrich explained in a 2016 article in *Saveur*:

Confirmation that feaguing and "cock-tail" are indeed related is provided by a little piece of political satire printed in 1790 in a provincial English newspaper, in which the writer, deploying the term in (I hope) the figurative sense, claims that a certain clergyman "hath been guilty of monopolizing all the ginger and pepper in the neighbourhood, to make the asses who vote for Sir Gerald Vanneck cock their tails." That's also how "cock-tail" seems to be deployed in The Prelateiad, an almost impenetrably obscure Dublin verse satire from 1789, which refers to cayenne pepper's "cock-tail virtue."

Is the first "cocktail" actually a non-alcoholic ginger drink? It's possible. However, I admit that either way the definition has changed greatly since the late eighteenth/early nineteenth century. For most people, cocktails are a mixed drink containing alcohol. But, for me, cocktails are a sophisticated adult mixed drink. Period. It's as much the intent as the act of mixing. Alcohol is just one of the tools used in mixing them, even if it's been the dominant tool.

If we delve deeper into what a cocktail is, apart from the descriptions we've already explored, we can see that there are certain sensory components that become an essential part of its construction: intensity of flavor, texture, length, and piquancy. Those parts don't necessarily have to be the product of alcohol. Let's explore each one.

Intensity of Flavor

A good cocktail should be pungent, whether that pungency is from the spirit itself or the various ingredients. Let's put it this way: You never mistakenly drink a cocktail. You can recognize the intensity of flavor right away. You know what you're drinking, at least categorically.

Think about a Gin Martini: gin, vermouth, and orange bitters. Imagine lifting the glass to your nose. You can smell the piny-ness of the juniper, bright aromas of citrus, and warm spices. With each sip, there's a combination of those flavors but there's also a notable bitterness. The aroma, flavors, and bitterness combine to equal a force greater than other drinks. That's the intensity of flavor.

Texture

Now imagine an Old Fashioned. A combination of rye whiskey, sugar, citrus peel, and bitters, the very definition of a cocktail from 1806. It has a texture you can describe as rich, even luxurious. When each sip hits your palate, the texture is mouth coating and lingers well after the sip is swallowed. It feels weighty compared to water or soda.

Texture has to do with viscosity, which ranges in cocktails, but ultimately provides thickness. Honey has a lot of viscosity; water doesn't. The viscosity in an Old Fashioned comes from both the spirit and the sweetener. That combination is the vital difference in most cocktails between something considered watered-down and something with a substantial heft.

Volume

Volume can be described as the part of the drink reserved for alcoholic spirits. Lemon, sugar, and soda alone won't reach the top of the glass if you exclude the gin from a Tom Collins. There's an aspect of lengthening that happens with alcohol, apart from the flavor itself.

Spirits take up anywhere between 1.5 ounces, as with the Tom Collins, to 3 ounces, as with a Martini. You need to account for that loss of volume from the absence of spirits in non-alcoholic cocktail recipes. That may mean adding additional ingredients or just using more of the existing ingredients.

Piquancy

Perhaps piquancy is the hardest of the sensory components of a cocktail to achieve without alcohol itself. Piquancy, in this case, is the bite of alcohol. The finish that twists your face a little and makes you slam your fist on the table. Whiskey has piquancy in droves, so does tequila.

Bye Bye Mocktails, Hello AF Cocktails

When I was first planning to open Listen Bar, I spent a lot of time thinking about what to call our drinks. As someone who became a champion of not drinking because I love it—increasingly more so than I enjoy alcohol—I found most of the terms that describe the category dripping with disdain.

Mocktails took the cake. I would see the word on menus and feel like I had been relegated to the kid's table. Drinks under that moniker often seemed childish too—fruity, sugary concoctions that certainly didn't come across as counterparts to regular cocktails. No wonder the most commonly asked question from guests at Listen Bar is, "Which drink is least sweet?"

I was heartened to read Julia Momose's manifesto urging the industry to relinquish the mocktail title and treat the category with sophistication in name and form. We're long past the time of trying to "mock" regular cocktails. The best drinks in the category stand on their own and often require even greater talent from bartenders than alcoholic drinks. Nothing to mock here.

"Virgin drinks" is, shockingly, even worse. It doesn't just cast judgment on the quality of the drink, it also judges the drinker. The term plays into the false connotation of not drinking as a signal of being a prude. It brings up the weird cultural fascination with virginity and yet also how virginity is weaponized as a point of ridicule against adults. Then there's the disturbing history of alcohol culturally viewed as a social lubricant, aphrodisiac, the notion of "beer goggles," in contrast with the reality of alcohol as the biggest date-rape drug and its complicated place in the #MeToo conversation. In a more immediate sense, seeing "virgin drinks" on a menu suggests serving them to children, whose palates aren't fully formed, and implies you're missing out.

Hospitality, this is not. Nor is it a reflection of my experience with not drinking, which has been liberating, sexy, and thoroughly grown up.

Enter: the "alcohol-free cocktail." That's what we call our drinks. In the vein of the gluten-free, plastic-free, cruelty-free movements, the alcohol-free, or AF cocktail trend says a loud HELL YES! to removing alcohol by choice. It is not the lesser option—it is, in that moment, the superior drink of choice. Plus, how cute is AF as a cheeky shorthand. Take that, virgin diss.

Lorelei Bandrovschi
Owner, Listen Bar

To achieve piquancy with non-alcoholic ingredients, you have to understand that alcohol is an irritant. When, in your best Ralph Wiggum voice, you say, "It tastes like ... burning," that's because it literally does. But it's also astringent. What seems at first unpleasant is something that we consume in many ways, from the fire of hot sauce to the tannins of tea. Alcohol isn't entirely necessary to achieve this effect.

Low-alcohol drinks make it a little easier because they have some alcohol, but may need a boost here or there to give them the feel of a higher alcohol cocktail. Although you can also just lower the alcohol called for in any spirit or split it with a similar non-alcoholic ingredient. The Aperol Spritz does this well by cutting the sparkling wine with soda water. It actually makes it a better drink, too.

Putting it all together you can create something delicious and complex and hardly miss the alcohol, except for effect. But, to create a drink that rivals its alcoholic brethren, you will need to use a range of ingredients that embody the above sensory characteristics.

What exactly are those ingredients?

Chapter Two
If We Don't Use Alcohol, Then What?

Without alcohol, you might think it's hard to achieve the intensity of flavor, texture, volume, and piquancy that you expect from a cocktail. Those are the qualities that make a sophisticated adult beverage. But it's actually easy and becoming easier all the time.

First, there are a ton of ingredients that you can find in your kitchen that add those qualities. Some might even surprise you. Fresh fruit and vegetables, oats, apple cider vinegar, ginger, egg whites, salt, coffee and tea, to name a few. I bet you have some of those ingredients in your pantry or fridge right now.

There's also a wave of non-alcoholic spirits that has been growing over the past four years. As of my writing this, there are over one hundred non-alcoholic spirits according to spirits and cocktail writer Camper English. A drop in the bucket compared to alcoholic spirits as a whole, but still notable.

What exactly are they made of, if not alcohol?

No-alcohol "spirits"?

Whenever I've used the term "spirits" to describe non-alcoholic cocktail bases, I've seen staunch drinkers recoil. How can it be a spirit if it doesn't contain alcohol? And they're right, in a way. Non-alcoholic spirits don't fit the legal definition of spirits given by the U.S. Code: "The term 'distilled spirits', 'alcoholic spirits', and 'spirits' all refer to the substance known as ethyl alcohol, ethanol, or spirits of wine in any form …" Non-alcoholic spirits don't contain ethanol, or only a negligible amount of alcohol (under 0.5% alcohol by volume, or ABV).

Instead, the term "spirit" in non-alcoholic spirits is used to denote that it is distilled and/or operates in place of spirits. It's used in the same way as veggie burgers, which aren't actually burgers, and oat milk, which isn't really milk. They're like burgers and it's like milk. They're substitutes and a simple modifier, veggie or oat, does enough to distinguish them. When we say non-alcoholic or zero-proof spirits, it's clear these spirits don't contain alcohol but do evoke alcoholic spirits.

If they're not made from alcohol, what are they made from?

The short answer is water.

That's not necessarily a bad thing. Alcoholic spirits also contain water. Sometimes the water source is even a selling point, as with Scotch whisky's Islay peaty water or Bourbon whiskey's limestone filtered spring water. Alcoholic spirits can range as high as 95% ABV when coming off the still. They water them down to get to 40% ABV, a more common proof. You do the math.

And I suppose we've grown accustomed to buying water, but non-alcoholic spirits are not water alone.

Some contain a range of fruit concentrates, aromatic compounds, thickeners, natural flavors, coloring agents, sugars, and preservatives that are compounded to create a non-alcoholic spirit. Lyre's non-alcoholic spirits from Australia, which has a range of non-alcoholic spirits from spirit analogs to vermouths and cordials, is a great example of compounded products. Their Coffee Originale and Italian Orange are among the best non-alcoholic products I've tasted and are great stand-ins for coffee liqueur and bitter orange aperitivi, respectively.

Other brands use vinegar to create cocktail bases with a sharp bite, giving them an amaro-like feel reminiscent of shrubs, a traditional method of preserving fruits with vinegar. Examples include Proteau Ludlow Red—created by bartender and author of *Drink What You Want: The Subjective Guide to Making Objectively Delicious Cocktails*, John deBary—a combination of blackberry juice, fig vinegar, and extracts such as black pepper and dandelion with zero additives. And Sacré, made by partners Justin and Roger Branson from Woodnose Drinks on their family-owned maple syrup farm in Vermont using maple syrup vinegar, maple syrup, and coffee.

The processes used to create non-alcoholic spirits may even include alcohol at some point, as with Spiritless Kentucky 74. Kentucky 74 uses grain alcohol and charred wood under pressure and with a highly calibrated temperature to extract flavors you'd expect from barrel aging such as oak, tobacco, vanilla, and spice. The product is distilled with alcohol and then the alcohol is removed through a second distillation. (I work for Spiritless as the Director of Brand Education as of the writing of this book.)

Other non-alcoholic spirits using distillation include Ferigaia, a botanical drink produced in Scotland using local botanicals such as black currant leaf, chamomile, bay leaf, and seaweed alongside other sourced botanicals, and two exceptional gin analogs—Monday Gin, which is made in Southern California and has strong notes of juniper and a bitter bite, and Damrak VirGin 0.0, which is made in Amsterdam and has more citrus-forward notes.

Non-alcoholic Beers

I've become a beer drinker. But it took non-alcoholic beers to do it for me. Don't get me wrong, I love delicious craft beers. Farmhouse ales and sour beers especially are so complex and interesting. I also love a cold Bud Light at a baseball game or with Maryland blue crabs, two pairings that are near perfect. However, a beer lover I was not. First, I tried some of the new commercial non-alcoholic beers and was pleasantly surprised that they actually taste like beer. But then I tried Athletic Brewing's Upside Dawn and I was bowled over. Floral, citrusy, and hoppy, it doesn't win points for just tasting like beer—it wins points for tasting like a good beer. (I also love their All Out, a stout with coffee and bitter chocolate notes.)

Thankfully, there are other non-alcoholic craft brewers and even craft brewers with non-alcoholic labels, some of them well known craft breweries such as Brooklyn Brewery from New York City and Mikkeller from Copenhagen, Denmark. These are great options to drink on their own or good options to use in making cocktails or beer-tails, if you will. I also have an affinity for Heineken's 0.0., which is a delicious lager and great substitute for Bud Light when eating crabs or drinking at the stadium.

Non-alcoholic beers are brewed much like alcoholic beers and may even have up to .05% ABV, which I consider negligible but would be remiss not to mention.

A Comprehensive Guide to No- and Low-Alcohol Cocktails

No-Alcohol Spirits Are Just as Hard to Make as Alcoholic Spirits, If Not Harder

It took a lot of research to produce Damrak Virgin, taking two years to get the result we wanted. We tried vacuum distillation, membrane filtration, CO_2 extracts. In most of the methods we used, you lose the flavors, especially the most important fresh notes of the citrus.

We finally made hydro-distillates (water-based distillations) and that worked out, but it's still not a one-to-one copy. And It takes a lot of distillations to produce. For one batch of Damrak Virgin, it will take two weeks, distilling everything separately.

It is easier with alcohol. Oils from the citrus and spices, for instance, dissolve very well in high alcohol. Normally we use bags in the still for most of the herbs and spices. With hydrodistillates, because the ingredients are perishable, you cannot do that. Juniper berries and citrus peels get really mushy. If you put the citrus in water, it becomes soaked. The taste is bad. Soak it too long and it can cause bacteria, fungus. It is not just putting peels in a barrel. There is extra preparation time. You have to put racks in the still. Put the herbs and spices in there. Smash them a bit before or grind them.

We had to do a lot of test runs beforehand to get the results we wanted, but we are happy with what we produced. It may not be an exact copy, but in a way it is something even more special because of the time and effort we put into it producing it.

Monique ten Kortenaar
Head Distiller, Lucas Bols

Non-alcoholic Wines

I studied and worked as a sommelier and developed all the annoying ticks that many sommeliers have. I would drone on about Burgundy wine, terroir, and small production wines. I'd champion underrepresented regions. I was as likely to tell you about the soil composition as I was how the wine tasted. And I thought non-alcoholic wines were terrible, mostly because they were. However, I've found a way to keep some of the "charms" of being a sommelier and champion non-alcoholic wines. The reason: Bruce and Tammy Blosil.

The Blosils founded Delmosa Artisanal Beverages with the idea of bringing terroir-driven non-alcoholic wines to market, although I'd call them beverages because they can be made from everything from cider to seabuckthorn. (Terroir is the micro-climate and geography of a specific region but is also associated with traditional production techniques.)

These wines were anything but terrible. Delmosa's collection of non-alcoholic beverages mirror the flavors and ecological consideration of truly great wines. Take for instance Jörg Geiger's PriSecco "Aecht Bitter," a sparkling wine made from green hunter pears harvested in the Swabian orchards of Germany. To that he adds gooseberry, quince, wormwood, and bitter herbs. It's tart, fresh with notes of sweet orchard fruit, and a lingering but gentle bitterness. Geiger also makes a wonderful non-alcoholic bubbly with Champagne pears (a variety of pear). It's fuller and has notes of baked pears and pie crust with a mineral backbone and restrained sweetness. For another crisp sparkling wine alternative, made from chardonnay grapes, I like Thomson & Scott Noughty Alcohol-Free Sparkling Wine. Noughty has more dry elements starting with aromatics of phyllo crust and cheese, jicama, ripe green pear, and lemon.

There are many great non-alcoholic still wine alternatives, too. Jörg Geiger red- and white-wine alternatives are among my favorites, especially his red alternative Inspiration 4.7 with notes of dried chiles, blue cornflowers, raspberry, and pomegranate, and white alternative Inspiration 4.3 with notes of baked apples, celery, and white flowers, with a tangy finish. An Australian brand called Non makes the delightful Non #1, which stands in for rosé, with salted raspberry and chamomile notes.

There are other terroir-driven non-alcoholic wine alternatives, too, such as Éclat de Rhubarb, a slightly sweetened rhubarb juice by Brigitte Keszthelyi, and L'Argousier Pétillant, sparkling sea buckthorn and maple syrup, from La Ferme d'Achille Argouille. Each of these are highly quaffable and work well in "wine"-based cocktails.

No- and Low-alcohol Bitters

Bitters come with their own bite. They can add depth and piquancy to your cocktails. Generally, bitters are complex tinctures made from bittering agents, like gentian, peels, and spices macerated in alcohol. There are only a few brands that are making bitters with non-alcoholic bases (replacing alcohol with glycerin) but they still use some alcohol in the final product.

Fee Brothers, founded in 1864, make a range of mostly non-alcoholic bitters from Aromatic to Rhubarb. While they may only add trace alcohol to your final drink, some begin as high as 17% ABV. (Contrast that to the 35 to 45% ABV of most bitters.) If you're not drinking alcohol at all, you may wish to make your own bitters. Darcy O'Neil, a chemist and bartender, has created a great non-alcoholic bitters recipe that you can make at home. With a few modifications, I've included his recipe below that can last up to a few years stored in a cool dark place, such as a kitchen cabinet:

Non-alcoholic Bitters
Adapted from Darcy O'Neil
Yields approximately ½ liter

Bittering Agents
15 ounces water
1/3 ounce gentian
1/3 ounce bitter orange

4 drops cinnamon oil
2 drops nutmeg oil
2 drops black pepper oil

2 drops all-spice (pimento) oil

4 drops bitter orange oil

1 drops cardamom oil

1 drop clove oil

1 tablespoon caramel coloring

¼ teaspoon Polysorbate 80

1 teaspoon gum arabic

1/3 ounce white granulated sugar

Combine the bittering agents in a sealed container and let sit for twenty-four hours. Strain out the solids, reserving the liquid, and add the rest of the ingredients while processing with an immersion blender.

To find quality dried herbs and spices, visit Mountain Rose Herbs (mountainroseherbs.com).

For food-grade polysorbate 80 and gum arabic, visit Modernist Pantry (modernistpantry.com).

Salt Tincture

Salt is a wonderful ingredient in cocktails because it does two things. First, it suppresses the suppressor. Salt suppresses bitterness that suppresses sweetness. That means it ultimately makes the cocktail a little rounder on the edges, if you will, removing the bitterness but bolstering some of the sweet notes.

Second, it adds texture simply because you're adding more dry extract (the powdery substance that would be left behind if you put the liquid through a centrifuge). That enhances the body of the drink. What it doesn't do, in small quantities, is make your drink taste salty.

To make salt tincture, simply add 4:1 water to salt and shake until the salt dissolves. Use a good salt like Maldon. Transfer the tincture to a dasher or eye dropper bottle. You may also use a pinch of salt here or a pinch there, but the tincture blends easier and can be stored for up to a month in a refrigerator.

Acid Phosphate

Acid Phosphate is made of neutralized phosphoric acid and mineral salts, but is practically a souring agent. In that way, it is not unlike citrus juice (though it is flavorless). It was once a storied ingredient in soda fountains and, though it sounds antiquated now, you can imagine someone pulling up to the counter of a soda fountain and ordering a chocolate or cherry phosphate. And if you can't imagine that, imagine drinking a Coca-Cola, which has plenty of phosphoric acid.

The only brand I recommend is the Extinct Chemical Company's Horsford's Acid Phosphate, made by chemist and bartender Darcy O'Neil.

Teas and Kombucha

Tea is one of my favorite non-alcoholic ingredients because it encompasses so many different expressions and can be used in myriad ways. Tea itself ostensibly comes from one plant: Camellia sinensis. But, just like wine, tea is an expression of terroir. The geography, microclimate, time of year, curing process, and aging all affect the final product. I mean, there's Lipton tea, which could really come from almost anywhere, and then there's fifty-year-old aged Pu-erh tea made from a Da Ya tea bush in the Yunnan Province of China. They're the same plant, but not the same thing.

My one caveat is that, should you use tea as a base, you must over steep it to retain the flavor. A cold steep in water is preferable—really room temperature steep—for 30 minutes to an hour, as opposed to steeping in hot water. It will have less caffeine than hot brewed tea, be smoother, and fuller flavored.

There's also kombucha, which is fermented tea, sugar, bacteria, and yeast. Taking a SCOBY (symbiotic culture of bacteria and yeast), otherwise known as a "mother," you can create a fizzy, sour drink that oozes complexity. I will say, it's an acquired taste. But it can be delicious on its own or in cocktails. It's worth noting that some kombucha has alcohol but it will be labeled as such if it has over .05% ABV.

Fresh Fruit

Fresh fruit is a common ingredient in cocktails from Pisco-soaked pineapple cubes in a Pisco Punch to apple juice in a Tatanka (apple juice and bison grass vodka). In fact, it's so ubiquitous you might just overlook its tremendous value. When people criticize non-alcoholic cocktails, they often say: They're just juice. And sometimes it mostly is, but what's wrong with that? Juice is a component in hundreds if not thousands of cocktails. The Daiquiri, Margarita, Bee's Knees, etc. Don't sleep on juice.

And remember—fruit has other uses aside from being squeezed. For example, the peel. Several non-alcoholic cocktails that are Prohibition-era or before use lemon peels to intensify the flavor (the exocarp, or outside, of certain fruits is a factory of flavor compounds). Oleo saccharum is a "sweet oil" created by macerating lemon peels in sugar until they form a paste filled with intense lemon flavor. (See recipe on page 45.)

There are also purées that give more oomph to a cocktail in terms of flavor and body. Here I'm thinking about how pectin—common in all fruit—can be a thickener, adding weight and texture to a cocktail. Want more flavor and texture? Blend the fruit with sugar.

Ginger

For me, ginger is the greatest of all of roots. Used in medicine and drinks since antiquity, it's also inherent in the earliest mentions of the word cocktail, which I discussed in the last chapter. The gentle burn, or intense heat if you crank it up, is biting, as much as a strong whiskey in some cases. (Try some of the spicier ginger beers, especially Reed's Strongest Craft Ginger Beer.) That makes it ideal as an ingredient in non-alcoholic cocktails. I use it a lot. In fact, I think that having a good ginger syrup on hand is essential for making non-alcoholic cocktails.

Here's my recipe:

Ginger Syrup
Makes approximately 1 cup

1 cup white sugar
1 cup water
2 tablespoons grated unpeeled ginger root*
1 dash lemon juice
(Optional: A few dashes ginger juice**)

Simmer sugar and water together until the granules dissolve. Stir, remove from heat, and add grated ginger. Allow to cool. Add lemon juice and strain any solids. Stored in a refrigerator, this should last up to two weeks.

*Ginger root is so much easier to grate when frozen.
** If you prefer a hotter ginger syrup, add a few dashes of freshly squeezed ginger juice before straining.

Vinegars

If you want the intensity of flavor and piquancy of alcohol, vinegar can do it. Vinegar is a byproduct of alcohol, so it's not surprising that it carries some of the same characteristics. Also, vinegar has been used for a long time in drinks, especially fruit shrubs—a means of preserving the fruit.

There are tons of vinegar varieties and you can play around with everything from aged oloroso Sherry to coconut vinegar. There are also artisanal local varieties, among my favorites is Lindera Farms. But, overall, I prefer a workhorse vinegar, apple cider vinegar (ACV). However, not all ACV is equal. For mixing, I use Dynamic Health Organic Raw Apple Cider Vinegar because it's so well balanced. For something a little more mellow, though pricier, try craft producer Little Apple Treats Apple Cider Vinegar.

Exploring Flavor Without Alcohol

There's a thinking in many old bartending circles that you need alcohol to carry flavor and to create complex, nuanced drinks that stray from the "fruitiness" of mocktails. Not only is this not true (sugar, water, and vinegar—amongst others—are just as great at grabbing hold of flavor compounds), it misses the point on what can make no- and low-alcohol drinks so interesting. Of course, complex flavor mixes can be fortified with booze, but the truth is, recalibrating your formula and creating from scratch without focusing on the alcohol allows for new branches of creativity.

This thinking was actually instilled in me as a young chef in training, being taught that creating vegetarian dishes not pivoting around a piece of meat actually led to far more interesting combinations. Focusing on an ingredient and thinking about the aspects of it that interest you, or that remind you of something else, can be a great starting point. But trying to think about the end balance is also key. Alcohol brings structure, grip, and depth and a mix of simple, fresh ingredients can sometimes miss this.

One thing that differs is that often you're not using one crux-point ingredient. A simple and effective starting point for traditional cocktails is to assess the base spirit, then find ways of bolstering or contrasting notes that you find most interesting in the core booze. When you aren't using a non-alcoholic replacement as this center point, you have to layer flavors in a different manner (although you can of course use a fruit, tea, spice, etc. as this heart, and try to assess other flavor elements to highlight)—but rather than seeing this as a problem, it can act as to spur exploration in a new wave of flavor. You'll be amazed how ingredients behave when you start to stretch the ratios—using very low levels of sweetness or acidity, for example—and this new way of exploring flavor in no- and low-alcohol drinks will expand your application of flavor across the board.

Ryan Chetiyawardana
Founder, Mr Lyan

Verjus

Verjus is the juice from unripened grapes, red or white, literally "green juice" in French. (Picture biting into a sour green grape.) It's helpful to think of this less like wine and more like tart, fresh juice or even vinegar.

Like wine, however, the quality varies depending on the producer. You can get wonderful floral and partially sweet verjus or grapey and mouthwall-tearing verjus. One works well with cocktails, the other is better fit for salad dressing. I absolutely love Navarro Vineyards gewurztraminer. Made from gewurztraminer grapes, it embodies many of the floral and tropical notes you get from their gewurztraminer wine. In fact, it makes a great wine-replacement with a little bit of water added.

Fruit Syrups

I tell bartenders I'm training that fruit doesn't taste like fruit without adding extra sugar. Fruit syrups are just that: fruit and sugar. I know sugar isn't healthy for you in vast quantities, and I know that non-alcoholic drinks have a reputation for being too sweet, but sugar is still important for balance, texture, and flavor. You can always reduce the sugar and play around with alternative sweeteners, but I've found that products like agave syrup and honey have their own unique flavor and low-caloric sweeteners like stevia leave an aftertaste.

Fruit syrups can, as advertised, be made from just about any fruit. But some should be done through a cold infusion and others through heat. Strawberries that are heated have a very different flavor than strawberries from a cold infusion. I tend to prefer the latter and often dump sugar over a bowl of fresh sliced strawberries and let it sit until a sweet, red syrup pools at the bottom. Call me lazy. However, with persimmons I'm going to add sugar and cook them until they extract a dark, sweet syrup that pairs wonderfully with spices. Oleo saccharum (sweet oil) is a kind of syrup that uses the fruit rinds, resulting in a greater depth of flavor. It's especially used in punch recipes.

Here are recipes for a few common syrups used throughout the book:

Lemon Oleo Saccharum
Makes approximately 1 cup

4 lemons
1 cup sugar

Wash and peel lemons into strips, making sure to avoid as much pith as possible. Place lemon peels and sugar in a mason jar or Tupperware container and pulverize. Seal and leave overnight. The next day, stir and add a small amount of lemon juice to dissolve remaining crystals. Press and strain syrup through a fine mesh strainer. Discard the peels.

Lemon Syrup
Makes approximately 1 cup

½ cup sugar
½ cup water
Zest of 3 lemons (wash before zesting)
6 ounces lemon juice

Add sugar, water, and lemon zest to a small saucepan. Bring to a simmer and simmer until sugar crystals are dissolved. Stir, remove from heat, and combine lemon juice in the mixture.

(To make lime syrup, substitute lime zest and juice in the same proportions.)

Orange Oleo Saccharum
Makes approximately 1 cup

2 oranges
1 cup sugar

A Comprehensive Guide to No- and Low-Alcohol Cocktails

Wash and peel oranges into strips, making sure to avoid as much pith as possible. Place orange peels and sugar in a mason jar or Tupperware container and pulverize. Seal and leave overnight. Stir and add a small amount of orange juice to dissolve remaining crystals. Press and strain syrup through a fine mesh strainer. Discard the peels.

Grapefruit Oleo Saccharum
Makes approximately 1 cup

1 grapefruit
1 cup sugar

Wash and peel grapefruit into strips, making sure to avoid as much pith as possible. Place grapefruit peel and sugar in a mason jar or Tupperware container and pulverize. Seal and leave overnight. Stir and add a small amount of grapefruit juice to dissolve remaining crystals. Press and strain syrup through a fine mesh strainer. Discard the peels.

Strawberry Oleo Saccharum
Makes approximately 1 cup

2 cartons ripe strawberries
½ cup sugar
1 dash lemon juice

Wash, hull, and chop the strawberries. Add to bowl, sprinkle sugar on top, and pulverize. Allow to sit overnight in the refrigerator. Stir and add a small amount of lemon juice to dissolve remaining crystals. Press and strain syrup through a fine mesh strainer, discarding the pulp.

Raspberry Syrup
Makes approximately 1 cup

1 cup water
1 cup sugar
1 ½ cups raspberries

Simmer water and sugar together until crystals are dissolved. Stir, add pulverized raspberries (pulverize using a fork) and juice, and soak in syrup overnight. The next day, press and strain syrup through a fine mesh strainer. Discard the pulp.

Pineapple Syrup
Makes approximately 1 cup

1 cup water
1 cup sugar
1 pineapple

Simmer sugar and water together until crystals are dissolved and then stir. Cut pineapple in ½-inch squares, removing the skin, and soak in syrup overnight. Press and strain syrup through a fine mesh strainer, but keep the cubes for a garnish or sweet treat!

Celery Syrup
Makes approximately ¾ cup

1 celery stalk
1 cup water
1 cup sugar

Remove leaves and cut ribs into coarse pieces. Simmer celery ribs with the water and sugar until sugar crystals are dissolved. Stir and strain syrup through a fine mesh strainer. Discard the pulp. Allow to cool.

Notes:
(1) Sugar crystals dissolve even faster if you first add sugar to the blender and pulse

for twenty to thirty seconds, essentially creating superfine sugar. This works best for oleo saccharums.

(2) Fruit syrups usually last two weeks to a month depending on a few factors. They should be sealed air tight, stored in a cold, dark place—the refrigerator is perfect—and only opened for use. Look for signs of spoilage such as visible mold, off smells, and any discoloration. If any of these exist, discard.

Milk or Milk Alternatives

Milk is used in cocktails from Milk Punches to White Russians. (Here is where most people start talking about powdered milk in honor of The Dude, but I don't recommend it.) And it can add body, sweetness, and flavor to no- or low-alcohol cocktails. But you don't have to use cow's milk, per se. There are plenty of milk alternatives that work exceedingly well, including coconut, cashew, and almond milks. But my favorite is oat milk.

Oat milk is delicious (as far as I'm concerned), but it also foams well, one of the reasons coffee baristas use it in drinks like cappuccinos and lattes. The other good thing about it is that it's easy to make.

Here's my recipe:

Oat Milk

1/2 cup rolled oats
2 cups water
2 drops non-alcoholic vanilla extract
1 teaspoon cane sugar

Soak oats in water for 30 minutes. Add vanilla extract and cane sugar, transfer to a blender and pulse blend for 20 seconds. Strain through fine sieve. Discard solids. Store in a Tupperware or glass container in the refrigerator and shake before using. Oat milk should last 4-5 days.

Eggs and Aquafaba

Throughout the late nineteenth and early twentieth centuries, eggs make a big showing in temperance drinks. Take for instance Thompson's Spa Egg Phosphate, named after the famous Boston temperance bar. It makes perfect sense because eggs can add some of the texture that alcohol does. Plus, that foamy white head has its own allure–think of the crown of a Ramos Gin Fizz, stiff enough to hold a straw upright and teeming over the glass.

However, I've found the aquafaba works just as well. What's aquafaba? Chickpea water. From a can of chickpeas. Simply open the can and strain the liquid. (Use the chickpeas for a salad or hummus.)

Coffee

We love coffee. As North Americans, it's the third most consumed beverage after water and soft drinks. I don't think it'll be hard to convince you of its virtue as a non-alcoholic ingredient. And bonus: It gives you energy. The euphoria associated with drinking alcohol is one of the hardest things to replace. Coffee helps.

I would consider using unusual combinations with coffee, too. I've had everything from pumpkin to mushrooms. Baristas have created amazing signature drinks that use some of the same techniques and flavors used by mixologists. The key is to realize how different coffee can be from place to place, and by dialing in brewing techniques. Here comes the word "terroir" again! It's all the same bean, but coffee from Yirgacheffe, a small region in Ethiopia renowned for its coffee beans, might taste floral and citrusy, while a coffee bean from Brazil might be sweeter with chocolate and spice notes. Use those natural flavors to build creative drinks, matching the coffee's profile to ingredients that might pair well with it.

Also, drip coffee from a machine can taste very different from pour-overs, a method by which you slowly drip coffee through a filter (yes, slower than drip coffee; I know it's confusing). I suggest using the brewing technique recommended for the beans themselves and purchase whole beans whenever possible, grinding them yourself using a coffee grinder or spice grinder per use.

Chocolate

I love chocolate in its many forms, though I'm especially fond of rich drinking chocolate from Spain made with rice flour. Drinking cacao (cacao is raw chocolate) can also be brewed or steeped to produce a thinner beverage. Either way, I prefer using cacao to cocoa powder (processed cacao often has sugar added). And cacao, like tea or coffee, can differ from region to region. Explore!

In other words, when you think of chocolate beverages, there's a world beyond hot chocolate or chocolate milk.

Capsicum

Capsicum is the heat from peppers, usually in the form of hot sauce or a ground powder. I left capsicum for last because it's usually the first most people think of when they think of alcohol's piquancy, because it affects the same flavor receptors as alcohol. But it's also the most poorly applied. Too often people use it as a cheat for more complex, balanced flavors. Some spiciness is good, but it can also be a bit caustic.

My rule is this: no throat burners. Cocktails can be spicy, but they shouldn't engulf your senses in such a way as to render other flavors obsolete. Pouring ghost peppers on your tongue may be fun, or maybe not, but that's not a cocktail. Use capsicum as a supporting flavor, one that integrates into the drink, rather than hogs the spotlight.

Simple Syrup

Never buy simple syrup. As the name implies, it's amazingly simple to produce and costs pennies. Use white sugar, Turbinado or raw cane sugar (what I usually use), or Demerara sugar for special recipes. There are many complicated methods, but let me make it true to name:

Measure equal parts sugar and water, or 1:1. Weight is the best measure, but if you don't have a handy gram scale then volume can work, too. It's just less precise. Combine sugar and water in a saucepan and simmer until the crystals are dissolved. Give a stir, allow to cool, and bottle. Make as little or as much as you need, adjusting the volume accordingly. It should last about a month.

Chapter Three
When They Go High, We Go Low-Alcohol

Fortified Wines

Fortified wines are probably the single best base for low-alcohol cocktails. They're that magic place in between spirits and wine: They're both. And the ABV reflects. Some fortified wines add neutral spirits. Others are naturally sweet because the addition of spirits stops the fermentation (fermentation is the act of yeast consuming sugars), leaving behind residual sugars.

Fortified wines such as port or Madeira are hundreds of years old and have been used in royal courts and to toast the founding of nations. Some are common stock behind bars, such as vermouth. Others are a little more obscure in this day and age exactly because they can be complex, even if they've become darlings of bartenders. (Sherry, I'm looking at you.)

There are three fortified wines that I think are most worth considering for low-alcohol cocktails, though that doesn't mean you should feel like you are limited to these if you want to explore. Let's call it the fortified wine starter pack.

Sherry is my number-one call for fortified wines because it's so versatile. Really, Sherry represents a whole range of fortified wines from southwest Spain, including both the driest and sweetest wines in the world. And I use them all. Plus, they're commonly called for in classic cocktails—no need to reinvent the wheel.

There are seven main types of Sherry: fino, manzanilla, amontillado, palo cortado, oloroso, cream, and Pedro Ximénez (or PX). Fino and manzanilla are the driest (meaning least sweet), lowest alcohol at 15% ABV, and generally the palest in color. As you move up the list, there is more aging, more alcohol (17% to 20% ABV), and they're darker but not necessarily sweeter. If a Sherry is labeled medium-dry, cream, or PX, then it's sweet. (PX is almost sickeningly sweet, so save this to use in place of simple syrup or pour over ice cream.) For most cocktail recipes, I prefer the drier sherries.

Second to Sherry is vermouth. Vermouth is technically an aromatized wine. It's fortified with grape-based neutral spirits, but also includes botanicals, especially wormwood (or vermut in German). There are many types of vermouth, from vanilla vermouth to chinato, but the two most common are referred to as "dry" and "sweet." Those are the ones I use the most, and are most common behind bars. Vermouth can also be a cocktail all by itself. For an easy, no-fuss drink, pour sweet vermouth on the rocks with an orange wheel.

Don't forget to store your vermouth in the refrigerator. It is a wine after all, and the flavor and aromatics can start to diminish after a week of being opened. Though you may be OK with that and drink it for up to three months. Just know that fresh vermouth is the best.

Lastly, I'll mention port. There are a few styles of port as well, all of which are sweet. Ruby, tawny, and white port are ones that I often use. Ruby is the most common and tends to be red and grapey, while tawny is aged and tends to be more brassy in color and nutty in flavor. White port is made differently than the red port and, while also sweet, has a little more tanginess. If I bought one, it would be tawny.

Liqueurs and Amari

There are plenty of low-alcohol liqueurs and aperitifs ranging from 11% to 35% ABV that are great in cocktails. They're usually sweet and can be flavored with everything from fruit to flowers. Among my favorites are Aperol, Pimm's No. 1, sloe gin, and St-Germain, an elderflower liqueur. You can make wonderful creative cocktails with them or a simple spritz with sparkling wine and soda. Some of them are in classic cocktails, too, such as the Pimm's Cup or Sloe Gin Fizz.

Amari are bittersweet liqueurs, also considered aperitifs and digestifs. They can have complex flavors via ingredients such as myrrh—yes, the biblical one—and cardamom. Alcohol-wise, some are on the lower range of the spectrum, while others pack as much wallop as base spirits like vodka and gin. A few of my favorites are Campari, Cynar, and Brauglio. As I mentioned with cocktail bitters you use in small doses, these potable bitters have a bite that can mimic the piquancy of alcohol. So no need to go for proofy ones. You can create an entire cocktail list based on amari, which my friend and one of the best bartenders in the U.S., Sother Teague, did at his New York City cocktail bar, Amor y Amargo.

Shōchū

Shōchū is a Japanese low-alcohol distillate that is commonly made out of rice, barley, and sweet potatoes. It clocks in at about 25% ABV, but it can also be as high as 45% ABV. It's important not to confuse shōchū with sake. They're not the same thing. Sake is more comparable to wine or beer than a spirit.

Shōchū makes wonderful cocktails, and there are many different styles. (See sidebar on page 56.) Some are very flavorful while others can also be simple and clean in the way that vodka is, making it a blank canvas for flavors. One of my favorite drinks made with shōchū is the Chu Hi, a highball made from shōchū and soda. (The word is a portmanteau of "chu" from shōchū and "hi" from highball.)

Wine and Beer

Though it might outrage some snooty sommeliers and wine makers, wine is a great base to mix from. There are classic drinks such as the Claret Cup (Claret is British term for traditional red blends from Bordeaux), Champagne Cocktail, Sangaree, and many more creative takes. It can be a base, a mixer, or you can float the wine on top of a drink. And all kinds of wine are useful: white, red, rosé, sparkling wine, and dessert wines. But here's the rub: I wouldn't suggest mixing with one you wouldn't drink a glass of as the quality will show through. If you're looking to stock your liquor cart with a stash of low-alcohol mixers, throw in a dry white wine, rosé, red (generally more full-bodied), and good bubbly. They'll come in handy.

Cocktails made with beer can be delicious and convey an entirely different appeal than spirit-based drinks. They tend to be more savory and sometimes rich. I'm specifically thinking about the Michelada, a spicy "beer-tail." But there's also some more obscure beer cocktails like the Snake Bite (lager and cider) or Black Velvet (Champagne and Guinness). It's best to keep a few styles at the ready. Lagers are the workhorse and are the ones I used most in my recipes, but a good stout is a thing of wonder.

A Comprehensive Guide to No- and Low-Alcohol Cocktails

Shōchū Isn't Fussy

One of my favorite memories of shōchū takes me back to a smoky izakaya, where I am sitting at a worn wooden table. A bottle of imo (sweet potato) shōchū stands proudly above dishes of steaming dashimaki tamago, crispy gyōza, pickled cucumber, and slippery firefly squid. Next to the bottle is a bowl of clear ice, the glistening chunks chipped from a much larger block. In arms reach rest frosty bottles of Wilkinson Tansan, ryokucha (green tea), and oolong tea. This is the only kind of bottle service I will ever want.

Rokku (on the rocks), oyuwari (mixed with hot water), chawari (mixed with tea), maewari (rested with water), and sodawari (mixed with club soda) are some of the most popular serves of shōchū, and thanks to the relatively low ABV of honkaku shōchū (most fall around 25%, though legally they may be bottled up to 45% ABV), you can easily taste through all of these options in a night.

When I think of shōchū, I think of honkaku shōchū. Honkaku means authentic in Japanese. When you see this on a label, it means that it is otsurui shōchū—distilled once in a pot still from a ferment of kōji and one of fifty-four government-approved ingredients. It is the essence of the ingredient, an expression of terroir, and most deserving of its title as the national spirit of Japan. Rice, sweet potato, barley, and buckwheat are some common types of shōchū, but keep your eye out for date, chestnut, or even milk shōchū. I love to make cocktails with shōchū. It is how I introduce folks to the spirit and then I encourage them to try the shōchū neat or on the rocks. That said, the lower proof is not intended to be pasted into classic cocktail templates in place of another spirit.

Get a couple of bottles and explore the nuances of the various styles. Sip it on its own, with water, or and at various temperatures. Shōchū isn't fussy. Whether on an old table in a raucous izakaya, or in the hands of a skilled bartender, shōchū doesn't need a fancy framework in which to shine. It shines on its own.

Julia Momose
Partner and Creative Director, Kumiko/Kikkō

Chapter Four
Mixology Basics

Bartending equipment can be expensive. I have a particular fetish for it, and have as a result accumulated an army of specialized and antique tools. Anyone need an olive spoon—as if you needed a special spoon to scoop olives—or an oversized farm hammer to crush ice?

But lacking a full arsenal of bar gear should not be a barrier to entry. Below are some of the critical tools you need, and a few work-arounds. However, consider that while you can hammer a nail with a shoe, a hammer is still preferable.

I generally shop online at kegworks.com or cocktailkingdom.com. But I also encourage ordering from local stores, too. In Alexandria, VA, just outside of Washington, D.C., I shop at The Hour, which has vintage glassware and cocktail tools. (Some of the glassware has been featured in our pictures!)

Barspoon

A long spoon with a spiral handle and small bowl at the end is needed for stirring. This is the most useful tool that you have. Not only can it stir cocktails, but the bowl is generally 1/8 ounce and can act as a measuring device. It also suffices as a muddler. A long ice tea spoon can work but, because stirring requires craftsmanship, I'd invest in a barspoon, which ranges from $4 to $40.

Glassware

I'm a fan of the right glass for the right drink. There is not a lot that happens when you match the right glass to the drink as far as a taste experience but it does look better. And drinks taste better when they look better. Yet, I don't want you to spend all your money on glassware, unless money is no issue. Here are the six glasses I recommend for cocktails:

Double Rocks (10 to 12 ounces)
The Old Fashioned fits fine in an Old Fashioned glass but better in a Double Rocks glass, which is really a Double Old Fashioned glass, which is not double the size of an Old Fashioned glass but about one and half times the volume. Confusing? Just

remember that this is for strong cocktails with ice, or a single large ice cube, and rely less on mixers like juice and soda.

Highball (8 to 12 ounces)
The Highball is named after the drink, the Highball. Use this glass for drinks that are long, meaning extended by juice or soda, and served on the rocks. Also used for fizzes or drinks without ice, in which case a smaller highball will do.

Wine Glass (10 to 14 ounces)
I prefer white wine glasses to red wine glasses because they're not obnoxiously big. Red wine glasses can be over 20 ounces in volume when the wine, or cocktail, is a slim 4 to 5 ounces. Yes, you can swirl, swish, and note the aromas in the larger glass, but you can do that in a smaller one, too. Size doesn't really matter when it comes to wine glasses. Use what you think looks best.

Cocktail Glass (5 1/2 to 7 1/2 ounces)
The term cocktail glass is a catch-all term for stemmed glassware with angular or rounded sides. A cocktail glass that has come to prominence over the last decade is the 5 ½ ounce Libbey coupe. It's cheap, durable, and attractive, purported to resemble Marie Antoinette's bosom. A glass shaped after a body part doesn't necessarily add to the appeal for me. But the other reasons are sound. I also use a Nick and Nora glass, named so by bartending legend Dale DeGroff because it resembles glassware from the *Thin Man* movies, which usually falls in the same volume range as the coupe.

Hurricane Glass (20 ounces)
This glass is tulip-shaped and holds a larger volume, perfect for blended drinks. There is also specialty glassware such as ceramic coconuts, which I sometimes use for this kind of drink, and tiki glasses work for blender drinks, too. These are fun, though please avoid tiki mugs that read cultural appropriation—using sacred imagery or cultural icons out of context—and conjure racist stereotypes.

Pilsner Glass (12 to 14 ounces)

Lastly, a good Pilsner glass looks elegant and works for slightly larger volume cocktails. You can certainly use a pint glass as well, but the Pilsner is a little more sleek and attractive to me.

Ice

There has been much talk about ice in the cocktail renaissance. There are even ice companies and ice experts. Ice is important. It's the water part in the definition of the first mentioned alcoholic cocktail: spirits, sugar, water, bitters. But I'm not going to spend too much time on it. Usually, you have the ice you have, and it's smaller than cocktail bars use (we use 1 ¼ inch cubes) and less dense. To make up for this, there are silicone molds you can purchase that work wonderfully well. Or, read Camper English's blog, Alcademics.com, and you can recreate small glaciers in your home.

You're lucky if you have a refrigerator that makes crushed ice, but it's just as easy (as mentioned above) to scoop the ice into a Lewis Bag or folded kitchen towel and whack it until crushed.

Jiggers

You're going to need something with which to measure liquids. That something is called a jigger. They make different kinds of jiggers from bell shaped to conical designs. My favorite for home use is Oxo's steel angled jigger that resembles a small measuring cup. Doesn't matter which one you use at home, though professional bartenders usually prefer the conical jiggers. Just make sure you can read the measurements so your jiggering isn't a guessing game.

You can, of course, try counting. That's what bartenders in high-volume bars do. They raise the bottle with a pour spout, perpendicular to the glass, and count, treating each count as a ½ ounce. I tend to count in quick succession and treat the count as a ¼ ounce, making the count of six 1 ½ ounces. You may have to practice to get it right.

A Comprehensive Guide to No- and Low-Alcohol Cocktails

Mixing Glasses

To stir a cocktail, a mixing glass is needed. These come in many forms and are often decorative. The grand secret is this: You can use the larger part of your shaker. In fact, metal is a better conductor of heat and will chill your drink faster than glass. Some people will also use a weighted pint glass. I ultimately prefer glass mixing glasses because you can see what goes into them and they're more attractive.

Muddlers

My advice: I'm meh about muddlers. They aren't needed in most cases. The back of a spoon can crush most ingredients and, really, you shouldn't be muddling most things that hard anyway. Maybe to pulverize an oleo saccharum (see page 45), press the limes in a Caipirinha, or beat a Lewis bag (a canvas bag used for crushing ice) to get crushed ice. Otherwise, this can be last on your list. And especially don't buy one that has a varnish on it. That ends up in your drink! (Apologies to the muddle stick makers of the world.)

Shakers

Shakers come in a few forms. There's a cobbler shaker that has three pieces, including a built-in strainer. If you have one of those, it's likely stuck together and, despite banging it against the table, it won't budge. Professional bartenders favor a Boston Shaker, which is two cups: one small, one big. The smaller one is referred to as "the cheater."

A Parisian shaker is two cups but has convex sides on the top piece. It can be used somewhat interchangeably with a Boston Shaker, though it is sometimes larger. If necessary, you can use two large cups and perform something like the throwing method described below—pouring the drink back and forth. This works, but usually results in less dilution, so the drink will be stronger.

Strainers

There are principally three kinds of strainers: the Hawthorne, Julep, and tea (or double) strainer. The Hawthorne is typically used when straining a shaken drink. It's either round or square with a handle and has a coil stretching across the front, which can be pressed into the shaker to filter out ice shards and other matter with which you've prepared your drink, such as muddled herbs or fruit. If you have a cheap one, which is a lighter material and has a wide coil, it probably doesn't work as well as it should. If that is the case, I suggest an upgrade.

The Julep strainer is circular with a handle, but no coil. This strainer is used for drinks that are stirred in a mixing glass and where no solid matter is added. Lastly, the tea, or double strainer, is a fine-mesh cup with a handle used as a second strainer perched beneath the Hawthorne to catch any shards that make it through. If you choose only one, I'd make it a Hawthorne. It can work across the board, even if it's not a perfect fit.

Mixology Techniques

Like skinning a feline, there is more than one way to make a drink. Shaking and stirring are but two. They are, however, the most important two. While you can see James Bond ordering a shaken Martini—as wrong as that might be—even the least skilled among us instinctively knows that you shouldn't swizzle it.

My general rule of thumb is build drinks that are spirit and soda; shake drinks that have juice, milk, eggs, or cream; and stir drinks that are mostly or all booze. With no- and low-alcohol drinks you should do roughly the same. But let's replace "mostly or all booze" with strong flavors here, or drinks that more closely resemble boozy cocktails (see Aromatic Cocktails on page 216).

Let's cover the technique behind each one. I'll also touch upon rolling, and throwing, too.

Building
Some of the technical aspects might seem intimidating, but this one shouldn't scare you: Pour the spirit, add the ice, add the soda, and your drink is built. Often, it's helpful to jiggle the spoon in the drink afterwards but that's about it. My one additional piece of advice is to pour the bubbles into the liquid rather than on the ice. This will keep the drink its fizzy fizziest.

Rolling

A cousin of building is rolling. Rolling is when you pour the ingredients back and forth between two cups, usually the cups of a shaker. Add the ingredients and ice, pour between cups, and dump it all into the drink. This is the one time you're allowed what we affectionately refer to as the "dirty dump," pouring ice from the shaker into the glass instead of using fresh ice.

This technique isn't often used in making cocktails. The Bloody Mary is a notable exception, but should be used a little more freely in no- and low-alcohol drinks where shaking—a more violent action—would cause too much dilution.

Shaking

Shaking has become an art form. You should look competent when doing it but, to be honest, people also take it a little too seriously. I've seen bartenders shake as though it was a Tik Tok video in the making, but it really doesn't require choreographed dance moves. If you shake in any manner hard enough for 15 seconds, the drink will be sufficiently chilled and diluted. I do have some advice, however:

Don't shake it up and down. That looks rather silly. Hold the shaker parallel to the ground or at a slight angle.

Don't shake it with one arm. (That can cause a strained shoulder if you do it over and over again, night after night.)

Do hold it with two hands. Place one hand firmly around the base of one cup; the other hand firmly around the base of the second cup.

Do push and pull away, from and back toward your chest, with equal force.

Do engage your core.

Provided you adhere to my advice, you shouldn't look foolish when shaking.

Dry Shaking

Dry shaking is just shaking a cocktail without ice. This is most commonly used for egg or aquafaba drinks, where you're trying to volumize the foam. First you add ice, shake; strain out the ice, and shake again.

Stirring

While shaking is the bartending equivalent of a super collider—smashing ice cubes through liquid into the tin walls of the shaker—stirring is what Japanese bartender Kazuo Uyeda refers to as, "weaving together silk." It should be done gently but with enough vigor to create a small whirlpool atop the liquid. The best way to do this is by grasping the handle of the spoon between your pointer and middle finger and flicking your wrist with the back of the spoon bowl against the mixing glass walls. Do this for about thirty strokes. Taste. If it's too strong, continue stirring.

Throwing

Throwing is an older technique that was replaced by shaking. However, it still persists in parts of Europe and has become faddish in the United States because it's quite theatrical. To throw, you must use two cups. Fill one with liquid ingredients and ice. Lift that cup high in one hand and hold the other cup low. Then pour the liquid in the top cup into the lower cup, through a Julep strainer, creating a long stream between the two. Move the cups closer together, pour the liquid back into the raised glass and repeat. This method allows for aeration without as much dilution as shaking.

Batchology, or How to Make Drinks for a Party

Batching drinks is a way to have your cocktails done in advance, or partially done in advance. The ultimate batch is a punch, which will be pre-diluted with water and then you add ice—whether a large block or cubes—to chill it.

In general, I suggest thirty-five to forty-five percent dilution, though you may wish to shake or stir one drink with ice and weigh the pre-shaken or stirred amount (without ice) versus the final amount after shaking or stirring (also, without ice). Then determine the difference between them in terms of weight. That's the amount of water you want to add. Dilute accordingly and then the batch can be stored in a fridge and served from a pitcher.

A Comprehensive Guide to No- and Low-Alcohol Cocktails

However, if the drink calls for soda, batch the rest of the ingredients and then top with soda to serve. This will keep the drink lively.

You can also batch the ingredients without water and then shake or stir them to order. This gives the illusion of à la minute drinks, with the readiness of batched drinks. Either way, it sucks to have to make drinks à la minute for each person if you're throwing a party. You'll be bartending all night. Think ahead!

Garnishes

Not all cocktails need garnishes, but garnishes can be exactly what distinguish a cocktail visually from a glass of orange juice. There are six garnishes I use all the time, and come up with other garnishes periodically (e.g., burnt cinnamon on the Good Guy, see page 108). Overall, those six garnishes are somewhat familiar in their patterns and are as follows: peels, wheels, slices, herbs and flowers, cherries or whole berries, and olives. Be creative, but feel free to fall back on these six.

Peels

Peels are for when the drink needs a slightly sweet fragrance but you don't want to bury the flavor. My general approach is to cut the peels about ¾ inches by 2 inches with a Y-peeler and spray the peel's exocarp, or the rough surface of the peel, downward onto the drink. If the drink is then perfectly balanced, and might be thrown off by the bitterness of the peel (e.g. Dry Martini or Sazerac), I discard the peel after spraying. Where the bitterness either enhances or does nothing to distract from the drink, I will spray, twist, and either let it drop into the drink or set it on the edge.

And then there are those who burn lemon and orange peels by igniting the oils when sprayed. Cool party trick but, unless you're using a cigar match or lighter, you're going to get an awful butane smell or black streaks on the surface of your drinks. Save this for the professionals.

Pro tip: Trim the sides and cut either side of the peel angularly for a more finished and less rustic looking peel.

Wheels

Wheels are my version of the wedge. I'm just not a wedge guy. If the idea is to add a wedge to squeeze some additional lime or lemon into the drink, I say just add it beforehand. That's where the wheel comes in. It adds some aroma and looks beautiful. You could squeeze the wheel, but likely wouldn't be very successful in doing so. I also think thinly sliced wheels look more elegant than big unevenly cut wheels. This means: Sharpen your knife.

Slices

Slices are not wedges, but they kind of are. Take the pineapple slice. It'll be cut in a V-shape and you can even slice the bottom to stick it on the edge of the glass. Apple slices are another wedge of the slice world, though these can also be cut into half wheels and fanned on top of the glass. Strawberries can be treated the same way or just cut a slice in the bottom of a small one and affix it to the glass. Ultimately, it's fine (if you saw this coming, kudos) any way you slice it.

Herbs and Flowers

Herbs are perfect garnishes because they're aromatic, which adds to the complexity of the drink, and look beautiful in or on a glass. Mint and basil are my favorites because of their sweet herbaceousness, but there's always a place for a sprig of rosemary or some sage for a more savory aroma. Use fresh herbs for the most part and don't be shy. Whereas thyme might look better in a single branch, mint looks best as a forest of mint.

Bartenders sometimes slap certain herbs because doing so releases more aromatic oils. You'll see them slap the herb across the back of their hand or between their palms. You can also press a spoon against them or roll them before using them as a garnish. Don't get too kinky with this. No one wants someone's dirty paws erotically massaging their garnish.

Flowers are another garnish that are both aromatic and instantaneously gorgeous. Borage is a flower you'll find common in some old drinks, but any edible flower is fair game. Edible flowers don't just mean you can actually eat them, which is an essential part of the definition. It also means they're from a reputable food purveyor and not from a floral shop or grocery store where they may have been treated with chemicals. It's also not wise to pull them from the ground in the city. Dogs and cars may leave their spray in the form of urine or heavy metals; not a very appealing thought if you ask me.

Cherries or Whole Berries

Brandied cherries are a bartender staple. The bright red "maraschino" cherries you find on sundaes made from what theoretically were cherries and Red 40, a petroleum-based distillate, are an imposter. Don't get me wrong, they're delicious, but better left for ice cream than cocktails.

If you're skipping the brandy, try real maraschino cherries from Luxardo. They're dark and syrupy in the best way possible. They're not cheap, but treat yourself—you'll thank me.

Whole berries, raspberries, and blackberries make great garnishes. Stick three on a cocktail pick in varying order of color and they look fresh and enticing. Even better with a little mint behind them for color contrast and dusted with powdered sugar. Whether cherries or berries, the rule is usually one or three. Two is when you don't like the person on the other end of the cocktail (sorry if you're a frequent recipient of two cherries or berries, but it's time to evaluate your bar persona). Don't ask me where this rule comes from. But an old curmudgeonly bartender once told me so and I still believe him.

Olives

Frankly, I prefer olives on the side. It won't be shocking for those who visited my bar, but I don't really like olive juice in cocktails either. Olives take up space in the drink and are often plucked from a warm jar or tray at a bar and become little heat bombs in your cold drink. Use olives when the drink is a good food pairing to them. Spear them, fine. But you can also put them in a small side dish. There is no rule that says a garnish must be stuck to the glass.

"Secret of the Pros"

Before we get into the recipes, I have some pro advice. Cocktails are delicious when they're made with purpose and care. It's not just a technique or recipe that makes a great drink— it's an act of consideration; of love. If you wish a drink to taste perfect, you should shake one up with all that you've learned within these pages and then serve it to someone as an act of kindness or simply because.

Don't get me wrong: It's great to make a drink for yourself and sip it slowly, savoring each and every taste. But the truest sense of being a bartender is to give. That's what I love most about making drinks—giving to others—and I hope you do, too.

Chapter Five
No-Alcohol Cocktails

I started building this section by pulling recipes from both temperance books and old newspapers, alongside bartending tomes where some of the greatest bartenders have proffered non-alcoholic options. But I decided to keep it current, too. I either updated the old recipes or created my own using the sensory aspects of a cocktail in mind. In a very few instances, I kept the recipe as is. And I suppose a few got away that are not accredited—did anyone actually create the Sherry Colada or was it manifest from heaven?

In thirty recipes, I've demonstrated the way I've used the aforementioned ingredients in Chapter Two and outlined how you can do so as well. One easy method is just play Potato Head and swap out one ingredient for a similar ingredient: grapefruit juice for lemon, honey for simple syrup, etc. In some cases, you may think a cocktail is too tart or too sweet. There's nothing stopping you from adjusting the recipes for your own tastes. We all live in our own perceptual world, as Master of Wine Tim Hanni once told me. Everyone is entitled to their tastes. Cocktails are finicky things. If one recipe was perfect, no other bartending guide or recipe book would be needed. That's why it's worth noting changes and trying to adjust the syrup or citrus or bitters. However, I've worked long and hard on this, so my recipes are actually perfect, thank you.

You may notice that some of the ingredients, as previously discussed in Chapter Two, actually contain trace amounts of alcohol. Sometimes fruit contains trace alcohol, too, but that's beside the point. I promised choices and here are choices. Using grocery ingredients and not premade bitters or dealcoholized wine or beer will help avoid any alcohol not natural to the product.

As I pointed out in the Introduction, you can spike some of these with low amounts of alcohol if you so wish. But when you change them in that way, you are the author and I bear no responsibility for the recipe being a failure. Have at it, but don't have at me. I am blameless. I made the recipes to stand on their own except where otherwise noted.

A Comprehensive Guide to No- and Low-Alcohol Cocktails

The Brunswick Cooler shows up in old cocktail books like the 1895 *Modern American Drinks: How to Mix and Serve All Kinds of Cups and Drinks* by George J. Kappeler. It's basically a lemonade and ginger ale with the addition of the peel. But, oh, is that peel important. From the Rickey to the Brunswick Cooler, citrus peels can add aromatics and bitterness to the drink.

Brunswick Cooler

Makes 1 drink
Serve in a highball glass

1 lemon
2 ounces lemon juice
1 ounce ginger syrup (see page 41)
½ ounce lemon syrup (see page 45)
3 ounces soda water

Cut one long spiral from the lemon and wrap around inside of highball glass. In a shaker, combine lemon juice, ginger syrup, and lemon syrup with ice and shake vigorously. Strain liquid into highball glass with spiral, add fresh ice, top with soda, and give it a gentle stir before serving.

I'm obsessed with Rickeys. They are the official drink of my city, Washington, D.C., after all (with a little lobbying from me). The original Rickey was made with Bourbon and, later, gin. But the Lime Rickey and Cherry Lime Rickey ended up just as famous as soda fountain drinks, with many people having fond childhood memories of the non-alcoholic versions. But these non-alcoholic Rickeys are for anyone who loves delicious drinks, and it's as perfect as the alcoholic version on a hot summer day.

Cherry Lime Rickey

Makes 1 drink
Serve in a highball glass

1 ¼ ounces fresh lime juice
½ ounce sour cherry juice
¼ ounce pineapple syrup (see page 47)
Shell of half of a lime
4 ounces sparkling mineral water

In a shaker, combine the lime juice, sour cherry juice, and pineapple syrup with ice and shake vigorously. Place the lime shell in the highball glass, then strain liquid into the glass. Add fresh ice, top with sparkling mineral water, and give it a gentle stir.

A Comprehensive Guide to No- and Low-Alcohol Cocktails

The Horse's Neck is an old non-alcoholic drink; basically, a ginger ale with a lemon peel. Adding grapefruit and lemon juice makes it far better. The bitters are not entirely necessary but do add a kick.

GF
Horse's Neck

Makes 1 drink
Serve in a highball glass

1 grapefruit
1 ¼ ounces fresh grapefruit juice
¾ ounces fresh lemon juice
1 ounce ginger syrup (see page 41)
6 drops of salt tincture (see page 38)
3 ounces soda water
1 dash non-alcoholic bitters (optional)

Cut one long spiral from a grapefruit and wrap around inside of highball glass (save grapefruit to juice). In a shaker, combine grapefruit and lemon juices, ginger syrup, bitters, and salt tincture with ice and shake vigorously. Strain liquid into highball glass with spiral, add fresh ice, and top with soda.

A Comprehensive Guide to No- and Low-Alcohol Cocktails

What this julep has to do with Havana I couldn't tell you. It was created in the early twentieth century and is a lovely julep with a Champagne-like elegance from the sparkling wine. Pineapple syrup is essential to give it texture and ground the drink. Otherwise, it might just float away on the bubbles. You can reduce the syrup if your non-alcoholic sparkling wine is on the sweet side.

Havana Julep

Makes 1 drink
Serve in a julep cup or double rocks glass

½ ounce fresh lemon juice
¾ ounce fresh grapefruit juice
1 ounce pineapple syrup (see page 47)
6 drops salt tincture (see page 38)
2 ounces non-alcoholic sparkling wine
Crushed ice
4 mint sprigs, 1 pineapple slice, and a pinch of ground nutmeg for garnish

In a shaker, combine lemon juice, grapefruit juice, pineapple syrup, and salt tincture with ice and shake vigorously. Strain liquid into a julep cup or double rocks glass, add sparkling wine, then add crushed ice. Garnish with mint sprigs and pineapple slice, and sprinkle ground nutmeg over the top.

A Comprehensive Guide to No- and Low-Alcohol Cocktails

This drink follows Blackberry Punch, Blackberry Punch No. 1, and Blackberry Punch No. 2. from *On Uncle Sam's Water Wagon*, a non-alcoholic recipe book from 1919. The older recipes call for salt, which proves that salt is nothing new in drinks. To that, I added aquafaba and ginger syrup. It's a refreshing drink, served individually or batched.

Blackberry Punch No. 3

Makes 1 drink
Serve in a double rocks glass

2 ounces fresh blackberry juice*
½ ounce fresh orange juice
½ ounce lemon syrup (see page 45)
½ ounce ginger syrup (see page 41)
½ ounce aquafaba (see page 49)
6 drops salt tincture (see page 38)
1 ½ ounces soda water
Mixed berries for garnish

In a shaker, combine first six ingredients with ice and shake vigorously. Strain liquid into double rocks glass and top with soda. Garnish with a skewer of mixed berries.

*To juice blackberries, add ½ cup of berries and 1 cup of water to a saucepan and bring to a boil. Strain the liquid through cheesecloth into a jar or container with a tight-fitting lid and allow to cool. Watch out for stains from the juice!

A Comprehensive Guide to No- and Low-Alcohol Cocktails

The Pinch Hitter is the canvas of the non-alcoholic sour. From this, you can experiment and try all kinds of variations. Or, as some bartenders are fond to call it, play Potato Head. Substitute grapefruit juice for lemon juice, add pink peppercorns to the ginger syrup, and you have a great non-alcoholic Grapefruit-Pink Peppercorn Sour. Try it as is, or play around and see what you come up with!

Pinch Hitter

Makes 1 drink
Serve in a cocktail glass

2 ounces fresh lemon juice
1 ounce ginger syrup (see page 41)
1 teaspoon apple cider vinegar
½ ounces aquafaba (see page 49)
6 drops of salt tincture (see page 38)
Thinly sliced lemon wheel for garnish

In a shaker, combine liquid ingredients with ice and shake vigorously. Remove ice and dry shake. Strain liquid into cocktail glass and garnish with a thinly sliced lemon wheel.

A Comprehensive Guide to No- and Low-Alcohol Cocktails

Based on David Embury's Southern Beauty in *The Fine Art of Mixing Drinks*, I decided to adjust it a little and name it after a line from one of my favorite John Prine songs, "In Spite of Ourselves." This zippy sipper is great for a hot afternoon as it's really just a souped up limeade with some aquafaba for texture, bitters for a little more complexity, and salt to add body.

Honey, We're the Big Door Prize

Makes 1 drink
Serve in a cocktail glass

3 ounces fresh lime juice
1 ounce lime syrup (see page 45)
2 dashes non-alcoholic bitters
½ ounces aquafaba (see page 49)
6 drops salt tincture (see page 38)
Thinly sliced lime wheel for garnish

In a shaker, combine all liquid ingredients with ice and shake vigorously. Remove ice and dry shake. Strain liquid into highball glass and add crushed ice. Garnish with the lime wheel.

A Comprehensive Guide to No- and Low-Alcohol Cocktails

The Temperance-era Griscom Cooler is a long drink made with soda. I turned it into a sour and used verjus in place of grape juice, which gives it more bite. The ingredients seem simple enough but, layered in the drink, give it depth. You can make it for a friend who likes Cosmopolitans or Clover Clubs and will be met by both with lip-smacking satisfaction.

Griscom Sour

Makes 1 drink
Serve in a cocktail glass

1 ounce verjus
1 ounce fresh orange juice
½ ounce raspberry syrup (see page 46)
½ ounce orange oleo saccharum (see page 45)
6 drops of salt tincture (see page 38)
Raspberries and mint sprig for garnish

In a shaker, combine all liquid ingredients with ice and shake vigorously. Strain liquid into cocktail glass and garnish with a skewer of raspberries and a sprig of mint.

A Comprehensive Guide to No- and Low-Alcohol Cocktails

Inspired by David Embury's *The Fine Art of Mixing Drinks* again—this time with his drink, the Pussyfoot—the Kitten's Whiskers is meant to be a simple, fruity, fun cocktail that is crowd-pleasing and easy to make. Use freshly squeezed orange juice as it makes all the difference.

Kitten's Whiskers

Makes 1 drink
Serve in a cocktail glass

3 ounces fresh orange juice
1 ounce fresh lemon juice
1 teaspoon grenadine
½ ounce aquafaba (see page 49)
Orange peel for garnish

In a shaker, combine all liquid ingredients with ice and shake vigorously. Remove ice and dry shake. Strain liquid into a cocktail glass and garnish with orange peel.

Molly Pitcher was a heroine of the Revolutionary War who brought water to the troops—via pitchers—and, when her husband fell behind the cannon, she is purported to have taken his place. A lot of this is steeped in myth but, regardless, her name has made its way onto cocktails and drinks. One was a temperance drink that has lemon, strawberry, and maple syrup.

Molly Pitcher Sour

Makes 1 drink
Serve in a sour glass

1 ounce lemon juice
1 ounce verjus (see page 44)
½ ounce strawberry juice*
¾ ounce maple syrup
½ ounce aquafaba (see page 49)
6 drops salt tincture (see page 38)

In a shaker, combine ingredients with ice and shake vigorously. Remove ice and dry shake. Strain into sour glass and garnish with strawberry.

*To juice strawberries, wash, remove tops and halve the strawberries. Press them with a muddler in a shaker or a bowl and then strain out solids. This is far easier with a juicer, but can be done with ripe strawberries and a little effort.

A Comprehensive Guide to No- and Low-Alcohol Cocktails

In many ways, this drink is what started me on my journey to look at old temperance recipes. It has a fascinating history as Thompson's was an entirely non-alcoholic Boston bar opened in 1882. The bar purportedly had a line around the block for this drink.

The verdict is: It's damn good, and a worthy replacement for alcoholic drinks.

Thompson's Spa Egg Phosphate

Makes 1 drink
Serve in a highball glass

1 ounce fresh lemon juice
1 ounce lemon syrup (see page 45)
1 dash acid phosphate (see page 39)
1 egg white from a small egg
4 ounces soda water
Lemon zest for garnish

In a shaker, combine all liquid ingredients except the soda water with ice and shake vigorously. Strain liquid into the bottom of the shaker without ice, dump ice, and shake dry. Strain liquid into a highball glass, add ice, and top with soda. Garnish with lemon zest on foam.

My former business partner and best friend, Angie Fetherston, doesn't drink. When I first served her a drink, she asked for a non-alcoholic cocktail. I made her a drink from Jerry Thomas' *Bon Vivant's Guide, or How to Mix Drinks*, an Orgeat Lemonade. She loved it, and it was then that I truly realized the importance of non-alcoholic drinks. Orgeat syrup is a sweetened almond syrup and can be purchased online.

Orgeat Lemonade

Make 1 drink
Serve in a highball glass

2 ounces fresh lemon juice
1 ounce orgeat syrup
1 tablespoon powdered sugar
Fresh berries and mint sprig for garnish

In a shaker, combine liquid ingredients with ice and shake vigorously. Strain liquid into a highball glass and add crushed ice. Garnish with a skewer of fresh berries and mint sprig.

The Lion's Tail is one of my favorite drinks. It's Bourbon, allspice dram (an allspice liqueur), lime, and bitters. It's spicy and fresh, a classic anytime-of-the-year drink. How to turn it into a non-alcoholic drink? Simple answer: falernum. Falernum is a syrup often used in tiki drinks that has ginger, clove, and spice. And it works, so we'll dub this drink the Lion's Paw.

Lion's Paw

Makes 1 drink
Serve in a cocktail glass

2 ounces fresh lime juice
1 ounce falernum
1 dash non-alcoholic bitters
1 teaspoon of apple cider vinegar
½ ounce aquafaba (see page 49)
6 drops salt tincture (see page 38)
Thinly sliced lime wheel for garnish

In a shaker, combine liquid ingredients with ice and shake vigorously. Remove ice and dry shake. Strain liquid into cocktail glass and garnish with thinly sliced lime wheel.

A Comprehensive Guide to No- and Low-Alcohol Cocktails

When I was in Marrakesh, I drank the most delicious mint tea that is served everywhere. In fact, it was so ubiquitous that my hosts often referred to it as "Moroccan whiskey." That got me thinking: Mint has a nice bite, and tea has some lovely structured tannins (the plant material that causes astringency and texture while tasting). Which makes it a good base for a mule, sans whiskey.

Marrakesh Mule

Makes 1 drink
Serve in a mule mug

2 ounces black tea (see steeping note on page 39)
1 ounce ginger syrup (see page 41)
¼ ounce fresh lime
3 ounces soda water
4 mint sprigs for garnish

In a shaker, combine the tea, ginger syrup, and lime juice with ice and shake vigorously. Strain liquid into a mule mug, add fresh ice, and top with soda water. Garnish with mint sprigs.

A Comprehensive Guide to No- and Low-Alcohol Cocktails

A friend of mine insisted I put an Arnold Palmer in the book, as if you couldn't figure out how to dump lemonade into ice tea on your own. But, thinking about it more, I realized that this drink could be tightened up a little by adding bitters for something more than the "Arnie Palmie Alert" alarm-triggering original. (That's a reference to the Will Ferrell and Mark Walhberg 2010 classic, *The Other Guys*, if you don't know.)

Tea Belly

Makes 1 drink
Serve in a highball glass

2 ounces black tea
2 ounces fresh lemon juice
1 ounce lemon syrup (see page 45)
1 dash non-alcoholic aromatic bitters
1 ounce soda water
Lemon wheel for garnish

Combine ingredients with ice and shake vigorously. Strain liquid into highball glass, add fresh ice, and top with soda. Garnish with thinly sliced lemon wheel.

I've heard switchel described as the Gatorade of the eighteenth century, used as a refresher for field hands. But we shouldn't be coy about it: It was often drunk by enslaved people. We just shouldn't obscure its terrible past as the pop-history of switchel often does. The drink itself is faultless and can and should be reclaimed by the modern drinker conscious of its past.

Switchel

Makes 1 drink
Serve in a Mason jar

8 ounces water
2 teaspoons apple cider vinegar
½ ounce pure cane syrup
1 teaspoon fresh grated ginger

In a shaker, combine all ingredients and shake without ice. Place in the refrigerator and allow to chill for at least 2 hours. When ready to serve, strain liquid into the mason jar with ice.

A Comprehensive Guide to No- and Low-Alcohol Cocktails

I created a cocktail with Pisco, an unaged brandy from Peru (and Chile), called the Salad Days Sour, which you can find in my previous book. That drink is so good that it deserves a non-alcoholic version. The original was named after punk band Minor Threat's song of the same name, so I went deep and used the title from another song they covered, "Sometimes Good Guys Don't Wear White" by the Standells. Toasted cinnamon makes a wonderful addition to this lightly vegetal sour.

Good Guy

Makes 1 drink
Serve in a cocktail glass

2 ounces lemon juice
1 ounce celery syrup (see page 47)
1 egg white from a small egg
1 teaspoon apple cider vinegar
6 drops salt tincture (see page 38)
¼ teaspoon ground cinnamon
Celery leaf (optional)

In a shaker, combine all ingredients except the cinnamon and celery leaf with ice and shake vigorously. Remove ice and dry shake. Strain liquid into a cocktail glass. Toast ground cinnamon with a pastry torch and sprinkle over the top of the drink into the foam. Lay the celery leaf on the top side of the glass.

The alcoholic version of this is the most popular drink I've ever created. Using blackstrap molasses, rum, and Cynar, it tastes like spiced maple syrup and tangy lemon juice in the best possible way. Chinotto has nothing to do with Cynar, except their Italian heritage and a few spices. Nevertheless, the orange-spiced syrup does the trick—it's hard to tell this one from its alcoholic predecessor.

NA Getaway

Makes 1 drink
Serve in a cocktail glass

2 ounces Chinotto syrup (available online or in specialty stores)
1 ounce fresh lemon juice
½ ounce maple syrup
½ teaspoon apple cider vinegar
½ ounce aquafaba (see page 49)
6 drops of salt tincture (see page 38)

In a shaker, combine all ingredients with ice and shake vigorously. Remove ice and dry shake. Strain liquid into cocktail glass.

A Comprehensive Guide to No- and Low-Alcohol Cocktails

I created this cocktail after drinking my favorite kombucha, which is made with apples. It's also partially based on a Pink Shimmy, which has gin and ice cream, but it's not as sweet. Yes, I know that's a rather circuitous route to get to this drink, but that's how I create drinks sometimes, in a way that's a little wobbly.

<u>Wobble Well</u>

Makes 1 drink
Serve in a cocktail glass

2 ounces apple kombucha
¾ ounce lemon juice
½ ounce grenadine
½ ounce aquafaba (see page 49)
1 ounce oat milk (see page 48)
Cherry for garnish

In a shaker, combine ingredients with ice and shake vigorously. Remove ice and dry shake. Strain into cocktail glass and garnish with a cherry.

A Comprehensive Guide to No- and Low-Alcohol Cocktails

This drink is an old temperance drink that I've tweaked so it's perfectly balanced, even with whipped cream. Whipped cream is an underappreciated ingredient. Yes, it's reminiscent of kiddie drinks; and, yes, that's the image non-alcoholic drinks need to reform.

But let's not throw out the baby with the bathwater. It works.

Old Glory Punch

Makes 1 drink
Serve in a wine glass

1 ½ ounces verjus
¾ ounce fresh orange juice
¾ ounce fresh lemon juice
½ ounce lemon syrup (see page 45)
½ ounce orange oleo saccharum (see page 45)
½ ounce pineapple syrup (see page 47)
1 ½ ounces soda water
Whipped cream
4 mint sprigs for garnish

In a shaker, combine the verjus, both juices, both syrups, and the oleo saccharum with ice and shake vigorously. Strain liquid into wine glass, add fresh ice, and top with soda water. Add whipped cream on top and garnish with mint.

A Comprehensive Guide to No- and Low-Alcohol Cocktails

To date, I've never named a drink after myself. But, what the hell, I created this Ramos Gin Fizz stand-in entirely alcohol-free and plant-based. And it's damn good. I'm sure Henry Ramos himself would approve. May my name go down in history as it goes down your gullet!

Brown's Cream Phosphate

Makes 1 drink
Serve in a highball glass

¾ ounce fresh lemon juice
¾ ounce fresh lime juice
½ ounce lemon syrup (see page 45)
½ ounce lime syrup (see page 45)
½ ounce coconut cream
1 dash orange blossom water
1 dash acid phosphate (see page 39)
3 drops non-alcoholic vanilla extract
½ ounce aquafaba (see page 49)
4 ounces soda water
Lime zest for garnish

In a shaker, combine all liquid ingredients except the soda water with ice and shake vigorously. Strain liquid into the bottom of the shaker without ice, dump ice, and shake dry. Strain liquid into highball glass, add fresh ice, and top with soda. Garnish with lime zest.

The name says it all. A recipe for this long beer-like drink appeared in *The Saint Paul Globe* in 1900, which I transformed into an aromatic cocktail. Hops are a great ingredient to use in non-alcoholic drinks, and this one is no different. I used Willamette hops that are spicy, floral, and fruity, used in English lagers and brown ales. But play around with different hops if you're a hop head.

Old Time Temperance

Makes 1 drink
Service in a double rocks glass

3 ounces ginger-and-hops tisane*
¾ ounce Demerara syrup (replacing Demerara sugar for white sugar in simple syrup at 1:1)
2 dashes non-alcoholic bitters
6 dashes salt tincture (see page 38)
Lemon peel for garnish

Add the tisane to a mixing glass along with the Demerara syrup, bitters, salt tincture, and ice. Stir until chilled. Strain liquid into double rocks glass, add fresh ice, and garnish with lemon peel.

*To make the ginger-and-hops tisane, heat 1 cup of water until it boils, then add 1 pellet of hops and three inches of ginger shredded. Allow tisane to sit for 5 minutes, then strain liquid through a fine-mesh sieve into a mixing glass and discard solids.

A Comprehensive Guide to No- and Low-Alcohol Cocktails

Smoky, rich, delicious non-alcoholic drinks are hard to come by. But Lapsang Souchong, a tea smoked over pine fires, is begging to change that. To the tea, I add some vanilla, lightly whipped egg whites, and a little ginger, which make it luscious and confectionary without being sweet. And there you have it: a smoky, rich Old Fashioned without alcohol. (The egg whites should be whipped lightly so they can blend with the drink rather than creating a foam.)

Campfire Old Fashioned

Makes 1 drink
Serve in a double rocks glass

1 egg white from a small egg
2 ounces Lapsang Souchong tea
½ ounce ginger syrup (see page 41)
3 drops alcohol-free vanilla extract
3 dashes non-alcoholic bitters
2 teaspoons fresh ginger juice
Orange peel for garnish

Lightly whip the egg white until slightly frothy and add to a mixing glass. Add all other liquid ingredients, then add ice, and stir until combined and chilled. Strain into double rocks glass and add fresh ice. Garnish with orange peel.

This coffee drink is based on the Vodka Espresso, also known as the Espresso Martini. The story about the Espresso Martini, created by famed British bartender Dick Bradsell, is that a model came to his bar and ordered a drink that would, "Wake her up" and "fuck her up."

In this version, one out of two ain't bad.

Wake Me Up

Makes 1 drink
Serve in a cocktail glass

3 ounces cold brew concentrate
1 teaspoon of apple cider vinegar
½ ounce aquafaba (see page 49)
Espresso beans for garnish

In a shaker, combine ingredients with ice and shake vigorously. Remove ice and dry shake. Strain liquid into cocktail glass and garnish with espresso beans.

A Comprehensive Guide to No- and Low-Alcohol Cocktails

Chocolate is a great ingredient for non-alcoholic cocktails because it's delicious and also mood-altering in the best way. Add some spice, and you have a drink that can rival booze drinks. My inspiration for this is Jacques Bezuidenhout's Aztec's Mark with Bourbon, creme de cacao, and hot sauce, but it could just as easily have been attributed to Mexican Hot Chocolate.

On Your Mark

Makes 1 drink
Serve in a cocktail glass

2 ounces spiced cacao*
6 drops of salt tincture (see page 38)
1 dash hot pepper sauce
Pinch of cayenne pepper
4 ounces oat milk (see page 48)

In a shaker, combine ingredients and shake vigorously. Strain liquid into cocktail glass.

* To make spiced cacao, add 2 teaspoons cacao, ¼ teaspoon whole cloves, ¼ teaspoon ground cardamom, ¼ teaspoon orange peel, a cinnamon stick, and 1 cup of water to a saucepan and bring to a boil, then simmer for 5 minutes. Strain liquid into a heatproof container and allow to cool. Store in a closed container for up to 48 hours.

A Comprehensive Guide to No- and Low-Alcohol Cocktails

The world needs more carrot juice cocktails. Carrot juice is a delicious drink in itself and pairs wonderfully with fresh squeezed orange juice. But it's a bit flabby without a dash of an acidulant, which confers a tart flavor (thus the acid phosphate). The turmeric honey rounds it off and makes a healthy but serious drink appropriate for both yoga retreats and bars.

Spray-on Tan

Makes 1 drink
Serve in a cocktail glass

1 ½ ounces fresh carrot juice
1 ½ ounces fresh orange juice
2 teaspoons turmeric honey syrup*
1 dash acid phosphate (see page 39)

In a shaker, combine ingredients with ice and shake vigorously. Strain liquid into cocktail glass.

*To make turmeric honey syrup, add a teaspoon of turmeric powder to honey syrup (made by combining both a tablespoon of honey and hot water). Mix thoroughly and allow to cool.

A Comprehensive Guide to No- and Low-Alcohol Cocktails

The name of this drink is the product of sheer laziness. It's too long to say Banana Daiquiri. This is the fun side of cocktails, which should be the only side I think about now. Non-alcoholic falernum syrup can be purchased easily online and has a spicy kick with ginger and allspice. You could easily make this a blended drink by substituting the shaker for a blender. Just add half a cup of ice and blend until smooth.

Banaquiri

Makes 1 drink
Serve in a cocktail glass

2 ounces fresh lime juice
1 ounce falernum syrup (see Headnote)
½ ounces banana purée (I use The Perfect Purée)
6 drops of salt tincture (see page 38)
Thinly sliced lime wheel for garnish

In a shaker, combine liquid ingredients with ice and shake vigorously. Strain liquid into a cocktail glass and garnish with the lime wheel.

A Comprehensive Guide to No- and Low-Alcohol Cocktails

Bloodied
Bullpen

I wrote this book in 2020, so the reference to the Washington Nationals' terrible season should be obvious to sports fans. However, while the Nats weren't exactly on point that year, this drink is. If you're craving a Bloody Mary and spiced tomato juice won't do the trick, add spiced beef broth. It's inspired by pho, but I don't want to claim it's something it's not. My friend Paul Taylor is the author of the broth recipe below. The brauthor? OK, I'll stop.

Makes 1 drink
Serve in a highball glass

1 ounce PT's Spiced Beef Broth (recipe follows)
4 ounces fresh squeezed tomato juice
¼ ounce fresh lemon juice
¼ ounce fresh lime juice
1 dash hot pepper sauce
Pinch salt
Pinch pepper
1 lemon wheel and 1 lime wheel for garnish

In a shaker, combine all liquid ingredients with ice and shake vigorously. Strain liquid into highball and add fresh ice. Garnish with lemon and lime wheel.

PT's Spiced Beef Broth
7 ounces fresh ginger (about one 14-inch long piece), peeled and sliced
2 yellow onions, peeled
1 bulb garlic, peeled
15 star anise pods
2 black cardamom pods
2 sticks cassia cinnamon
4 cloves
1 tablespoon coriander seeds
6 quarts low-sodium beef stock
3 tablespoons Kosher salt
6 ounces fish sauce
3 tablespoons white granulated sugar

Torch ginger, yellow onion, and garlic until the skin is charred. (Alternatively, you can place them under the broiler.) Dry fry star anise, black cardamom, cinnamon, cloves, and coriander until fragrant (be careful not to burn). Bring the stock to a boil and reduce to a simmer. Add charred vegetables and dry-fried spices and simmer for 3 hours on medium heat. Season with salt, fish sauce, and sugar, adjusting to your taste. Strain broth through bouillon or fine mesh strainer, discarding the solids. Freeze the excess stock.

The Virgin Pina Colada already exists. It's pretty much just coconut cream, lime, and pineapple juice. If that's what you want, I don't blame you. Go for it. I've ordered a few in my time poolside.

This drink, however, is a touch more complex, while still being fruity, sweet, and delicious.

Not-a-Colada

Makes 1 drink
Serve in a hurricane glass

3 ounces pineapple juice
2 ¼ ounces coconut cream
1 teaspoon Steen's Pure Cane Syrup
1 teaspoon apple cider vinegar
3 drops alcohol-free vanilla extract
6 drops salt tincture (see page 38)
Pineapple slice and frond for garnish

Combine all liquid ingredients in a blender with a ½ cup of ice and blend until smooth. Pour into hurricane glass and garnish with pineapple slice and frond.

A Comprehensive Guide to No- and Low-Alcohol Cocktails

I became obsessed with the Matcha Maca Latte at Calabash Tea in Washington, D.C., and drank it with alarming frequency, considering that the jolt of caffeine was jitter-inducing. Thinking about rich drinks people can make for the holidays, I decided to try my own version of that drink as a flip, a rich egg-white drink. It worked wonderfully and has now become a tradition. Rolling the glass in powdered sugar to get the look of snow drifts is a festive touch.

Matcha Maca Flip

Makes 1 drink

Serve in a cocktail glass

1 lime wedge

Powdered sugar

4 ounces oat milk (see page 48)

½ ounce aquafaba (see page 49)

½ teaspoon maca powder

½ teaspoon matcha powder

½ teaspoon agave syrup

½ teaspoon liquid coconut oil

Rub a small segment of lime around the edge of the glass and roll the wetted rim in powdered sugar. In a shaker, combine ingredients with ice and shake vigorously. Strain out the ice and shake again. Strain into sugar-rimmed glass.

A Comprehensive Guide to No- and Low-Alcohol Cocktails

This one is called Twelfth Night Cider and is from an old recipe but you don't have to wait until the Epiphany or even celebrate Christmas to enjoy it. This mulled cider is the best when leaves are falling, the weather is crisp, and you have dusted off your jackets in anticipation of fall's cool breezes. Basically, sweater weather. Heat it up and it's an instant warmer that fills the house with enticing aromas of cider and spices.

Twelfth Night Cider

Makes 25 servings
Serve in tempered glass mugs

1 gallon unfiltered non-alcoholic apple cider
1 vanilla from a bean that has been split lengthwise, scraping the seeds
3 cinnamon sticks
6 whole cloves
4-inch piece fresh ginger, peeled and sliced
2 teaspoons coarsely ground nutmeg
1 whole lemon peel
extra cinnamon sticks
4 baked apples*

Add cider to a large pot set over high heat. Tie spices in cheesecloth and add to cider, bring to a boil, and simmer for 15 minutes. Add baked apples. Ladle cider into mugs and garnish each with a cinnamon stick.

*Baked apples; preheat oven to 400° F. Add 1 cup of cider to a baking dish along with ½ teaspoon salt, 1 teaspoon ground cinnamon, and ½ cup brown sugar. Core the apples and insert a cinnamon stick. Bake for 30 minutes, basting with liquid.

A Comprehensive Guide to No- and Low-Alcohol Cocktails

Sober Entertaining: Lights, Music, Cocktails!

The point of a good bar, and by extension a good drink, is to unite and connect us.

In that way, a sober bar and its non-alcoholic cocktails should look and sound like any other bar in America. But, because people will put up with a lot more when they're drinking, a sober bar or non-alcoholic cocktail has to also transcend every other bar and create an experience. When you're sober, you're much more aware—your perception isn't skewed.

How do you do that in sober experiences: Create a moment where people walk away transformed? By designing those experiences with light, music, and color, and making sure to keep your audience in mind.

Lighting is so important. If it's designed for connection, the lights have to be up enough to see each other. But it's also about striking a balance. They can't be up too much. Music, too. When it comes to music, whether live or recorded, it can never be louder than conversations. Music wants to be the centerpiece, but not at mingling time.

And color, in the bar and in the drinks. I love drinks that have great colors and garnishes that set them apart. We drink with our eyes first before ever tasting anything. When we are looking at the drink, we're making judgments not just about the drink but about ourselves.

Sober entertaining is understanding that so much of what you offer someone is not just what's inside the glass but in conversations, in the people we meet, and in what's around us. A good space invites us in. We feel that we can drop our guard. People should walk away with new friends, which creates conversation and community.

Chris Marshall
Owner, Sans Bar

Chapter Six
Low-Alcohol Cocktails

In some ways, low-alcohol cocktails seem like a continuum of non-alcoholic cocktails. In other ways, they seem different altogether, and I debated doing one book or the other. Ultimately, I settled on the idea that choice trumps purity or consistency. That might make the next section more complicated and challenging to people who eschew alcohol entirely.

I have noted some substitutions you can make to create a non-alcoholic cocktail with all the previous caveats discussed in Chapter Five. Some of them are dead ringers for the alcoholic version, and you won't miss a thing if you make the substitution as indicated.

I've also listed the amount of alcohol by volume, or ABV, so that you can decide in that way whether a cocktail is appropriate for you. The ABV for these drinks ranges from 2% to 13%—that's quite a range! Thirteen percent is pretty high and as much alcohol as a glass of some red wines but, compared to boozier drinks such as the Manhattan or Old Fashioned, is nearly half of the alcohol. Therefore, low-alcohol is relative in this book. Obviously, two or three glasses of a cocktail with an ABV of 13% can very well put some people on their Adonises.

The formula I used to calculate the ABV was cribbed from a blog post made by Darcy O'Neil on his blog ArtofDrink.com, who is also the author of our nonalcoholic bitters recipe. (See page 37) In math terms, it's as follows:

[Volume of Strongest ABV Ingredient x strongest ingredient's ABV% + Volume of Modifying Alcohol Ingredient x modifying ingredient's ABV%] / Sum Volume of Ingredients (including dilution) x 100

Taking the first cocktail recipe as a starting point, that math is as follows:

[2 ounces dry amontillado Sherry x 17% ABV + 1 ounce sweet vermouth x 22% ABV] / 4.35 ounces (including 45% dilution, or 1.35 ounces water) x 100 = 13% ABV Or: [2 x .34 + 1 x .25] / 4.35 x 100 = 12.8735632

This thoroughly exhausts my knowledge of math, but I hope it gives you a tool to use when determining the ABV of beverages.

The Chu-hi is one Japan's most popular drinks. Shōchū makes a great base for this highball—get it, chu from Shōchū and hi from highball—and can be flavored with virtually any fruit. I like the grapefruit version and a touch of acid phosphate. That keeps it light and tangy.

Don't expect a lot of flavor from this drink; it's meant to be light drinking.

GF
Chu-hi

Makes 1 drink
Serve in a highball glass
9% ABV

1 ½ ounces Shōchū
½ ounce grapefruit oleo saccharum (see page 46)
1 dash acid phosphate (see page 39)
4 ounces soda water
Pink grapefruit peel for garnish

Combine Shōchū, pink grapefruit oleo saccharum, and the acid phosphate in highball glass and stir until combined. Add ice and top with soda water. Garnish with pink grapefruit peel.

A few years back, a food writer argued that the Aperol Spritz was a terrible drink. The problem is—for such a terrible drink—it's actually very popular, and she felt the sting of being ratioed. Not that I condone the ratio-ing. It's just a drink, after all. But the public has spoken. Say what you want about the Aperol Spritz, just know that you may hold that opinion alone.

Aperol Spritz

Makes 1 drink
Serve in a wine glass
12% ABV

3 ounces dry brut prosecco (or Thomson & Scott Noughty Alcohol-Free Sparkling Chardonnay)
2 ounces Aperol (or Lyre's Italian Orange)
1 ounce soda water
Thinly sliced orange wheel for garnish

Pour brut prosecco and Aperol in a wine glass. Add ice and top with soda water. Garnish with thinly sliced orange wheel.

A Comprehensive Guide to No- and Low-Alcohol Cocktails

I've already accepted Sprite in a Pimm's Cup, so you're welcome to include it in this drink as well. It's tasty. But the drink will be far better with a bitter lemon soda such as Fever Tree's Bitter Lemon.

Rebujito

Makes 1 drink
Serve in a highball
5% ABV

2 ounces fino Sherry
4 ounces lemon soda
Lemon peel for garnish

Add Sherry to highball glass, add ice, and top with lemon-lime soda. Garnish with lemon peel.

This is an easy drink that charms just about everyone. I might even suggest making pitchers for an afternoon with friends, preferably one where you have nowhere to be. It's also easy to substitute non-alcoholic bubbly for an even lower alcohol drink.

St. Germain Cocktail

Makes 1 drink
Serve in a highball glass
10% ABV

1 ½ ounces St-Germain elderflower liqueur (or Elderflower Syrup)
2 ounces dry sparkling wine (or Thomson & Scott Noughty Alcohol-Free Sparkling Chardonnay; see page 36)
2 ounces soda water
Lemon peel for garnish

Combine all liquid ingredients in a highball glass, add ice, and stir. Garnish with lemon peel.

A Comprehensive Guide to No- and Low-Alcohol Cocktails

My sour cherry version of the Kir, not to be confused with Kir Royales, in which you can substitute sparkling wine, non-alcoholic or regular. This drink is fresh and tart. It makes a lovely start to a meal or an easy cocktail for a dinner party when you want something that looks good, tastes good, and doesn't require a million ingredients.

We'll Never Be Royales

Makes 1 drink
Serve in a cocktail glass
11% ABV

4 ounces aligoté or other dry white wine (or Jörg Geiger Inspiration 4.3; see page 36)
¼ ounce sour cherry juice concentrate
Lime wheel

Combine all liquid ingredients in a cocktail glass and gently stir.

A Comprehensive Guide to No- and Low-Alcohol Cocktails

Not to be confused with the espresso drink, an Americano cocktail is basically a Negroni lite. Instead of gin, you use soda water, which greatly reduces the proof. It also makes it a perfect drink to sip at a café on a sunny afternoon in Venice, Italy. Or to have in your backyard, dipping your feet in a baby pool. The less sexy but equally satisfying substitute.

Americano

Makes 1 drink
Serve in a highball glass
12% ABV

1 ½ ounces Campari (or Lyre's Italian Orange)
1 ½ ounces sweet vermouth (or Lyre's Aperitif Rosso)
3 ounces soda water
Orange peel

Pour Campari and sweet vermouth into a highball glass. Add ice and top with soda water. Garnish with orange peel.

A Comprehensive Guide to No- and Low-Alcohol Cocktails

Though Champagne conjures up visions of celebration, glitz, and glamour, it's also a delicious anytime drink. And it makes an excellent cocktail ingredient. So don't feel that you have to drink Champagne on a special occasion and by itself only.

This Champagne "Old Fashioned" is for any occasion.

Champagne Cocktail

Makes 1 drink
Serve in a wine glass
12% ABV

1 sugar cube
6 dashes aromatic bitters
4 ounces brut Champagne (or Jörg Geiger Birnenschaumwein; see page 36)
Lemon peel for garnish

Coat a sugar cube with bitters and add to the wine glass. Pour chilled Champagne over and garnish with lemon peel.

A Comprehensive Guide to No- and Low-Alcohol Cocktails

The Bellini is endlessly praised and frequently criticized. It's delicious, but too often it's made from artificial ingredients instead of fresh white peaches whose window is four to six weeks out of the year. Since the Bellini was named after the artist, I dedicated my mango-and-passionfruit riff to "other famous painters."

<u>Other Famous Painters</u>

Makes 1 drink
Serve in a wine glass
6% ABV

2 ounces brut prosecco (or Thomson & Scott Noughty Alcohol-Free Sparkling Chardonnay; see page 36)
2 ounces soda water
1 ounce mango purée (I use The Perfect Purée)
½ ounces passion fruit purée (I use The Perfect Purée)
Mango slice for garnish (optional)

Combine liquid ingredients in a wine glass and stir until combined. Add ice. Garnish with mango slice.

A Comprehensive Guide to No- and Low-Alcohol Cocktails

This is a white-wine riff on the sangaree, but with fresh, springtime ingredients. I imagine that this is the kind of drink most people will not object to—that would be like objecting to puppies, sunshine, and daffodils. It's a safe drink, in other words… OK, you got it.

Safe Word

Makes 1 drink
Serve in a wine glass
9% ABV

4 ounces riesling (or Navarro Vineyards Gewürztraminer Verjus; see page 44)
½ ounce strawberry oleo saccharum (see page 46)
1 dash fresh lemon juice
Thinly sliced lemon wheel and 1 sprig thyme for garnish

Combine all liquid ingredients in wine glass, add ice, and stir. Garnish with thinly sliced lemon wheel and thyme sprig.

A Comprehensive Guide to No- and Low-Alcohol Cocktails

There's a Shandy, made with beer and lemonade, and there's a Pimm's Cup, made with Pimm's Cup No. 1 and lemon soda. Both very British drinks. With little regard for propriety or the crown, as an obnoxious American, I combined them.

But it's a great springtime drink that, despite my impropriety, may very well earn me knighthood.

Squash 57

Makes 1 drink
Serve in a Pilsner glass
2% ABV

1 ounce Pimm's Cup No. 1
3 ounces fresh lemon juice
2 ounces lemon syrup (see page 45)
6 ounces crisp lager (or Heineken 0.0; see page 33)
1 mint sprig and a lemon wheel for garnish

In a shaker, combine Pimm's, lemon juice, and lemon syrup with ice and shake vigorously. Strain liquid into pilsner glass, add fresh ice, and top with beer. Garnish with mint sprig and lemon wheel.

A common Portuguese drink is white port and tonic. Very refreshing and very simple. Squeezing a little blackberry juice and adding a rosemary sprig ups the flavor ante (and presentation), and offers a drink that's both attractive and tastes great.

Never Have I Ever

Makes 1 drink
Serve in a double rocks glass
5% ABV

1 ½ ounces white port
¼ ounce blackberry juice
4 ounces tonic water
Rosemary sprig and fresh berries for garnish

Combine port and blackberry juice in double rocks glass with ice. Top with tonic water and garnish with rosemary sprig and berries.

BARGAIN LANE - HOLLAND
910 CHICAGO DRIVE
HOLLAND MI 49423
5824751092

Cashier: Helene H
101.E13p 5052 2 13:191

Change	$0.85
Cash (tendered)	$70.00
CASH SALE	$69.95
Total	$69.95
Michigan State Tax	$0.30
Subtotal	$69.00
Pull 15.9? R	$69.95

EBREV/VOLEY/OMER
Onibe pub/Wclover comb

RAYMCOLL IBE/VOLEY/OMER
CLOVER IO OLKME IY3VYCEU

 Asean/Wclover comb/pub qu
Clover Y asean benyel

BARGAIN LANE - HOLLAND

710 CHICAGO DRIVE
HOLLAND, MI 49423

2604159245

Cashier: Helene H.

25-Feb-2025 2:13:16P

6 $1 Bin	$6.00

| **Subtotal** | **$6.00** |
| Michigan State Tax   6% | $0.36 |

| **Total** | **$6.36** |

CASH SALE	$6.36
Cash tendered	$7.00
Change	$0.64

Online: https://clover.com/p
/EJREVAOEYOWER

Clover ID: QTKWEI737VCEO

Payment EJREVAOEYOWER

I'm happy to say that this drink has served me well over the last decade. It's a riff on the sangria—not sangaree—using white wine and melon. And it works for exactly the same reason as sangria: It's refreshing, colorful, and light. The frozen melon balls are beautiful in the glass, but they also slowly melt and add flavor. The basil garnish is essential to aromatize the drink. Use a melon baller to scoop out small watermelon, cantaloupe, and honeydew melon balls and then freeze them (I found it easiest to put these in an ice tray).

Melon-Basil Cup

Makes 1 drink
Serve in a wine glass
10% ABV

3 ounces dry white wine (or Navarro Vineyards Gewürztraminer Verjus; see page 44)
½ ounce orange oleo saccharum (see page 45)
1 dash fresh lemon juice
1 teaspoon honey syrup*
Melon Balls
1 sprig basil for garnish

Combine liquid ingredients in a wine glass and gently stir. Add frozen melon balls in place of ice. Garnish with basil sprig.

*To make honey syrup, add 2 parts honey to 1 part boiling water, stir, and allow to cool before using.

This drink is a little weird, and that's why I love it. The botanicals, dry Champagne, and sweet cola, all conjure a drink that is at once both familiar and strange. Add some drops of absinthe and it's complete.

This drink is not for everyone, but I suspect for some it scratches just the right itch.

Team Player

Makes 1 drink
Serve in a double rocks glass
8% ABV

2 ounces dry vermouth
2 ounces Coca-Cola
1 ounce brut Champagne
1 ounce soda water
3 dashes absinthe
Thinly sliced lime wheel for garnish

Combine all liquid ingredients in highball glass with ice and stir until chilled. Strain liquid into double rocks glass and add fresh ice. Garnish with thinly sliced lime wheel.

There really is a Hemingway Look-a-Like Contest at Sloppy Joe's bar in Key West, Florida. There, the Ernest Hemingway papa-icon of choice is not the slender soldier from Italy or the rugged bullfighter of Spain, but the chubby man in a cable knit sweater and full Santa beard.

If that's the papa doble image that conjures the Papa Doble drink with rum, think of this drink as the slimmer version, also sans sugar but with some bubbles.

Hemingway Lookalike

Makes 1 drink
Serve in a cocktail glass
6% ABV

2 ounces fresh grapefruit juice
½ ounce fresh lime juice
½ ounce maraschino liqueur
1 dash grapefruit bitters
2 ounces dry sparkling wine
Grapefruit peel for garnish

Combine the juices, maraschino liqueur, and bitters in a mixing glass with ice and stir. Strain liquid into cocktail glass, top with sparkling wine, and garnish with grapefruit peel.

The Pimm's Cup is sometimes made with ginger ale and sometimes made with lemon soda. The ginger version better resonates with me and adding a squeeze of lemon gives it just the perfect amount of tartness. Though I'll accept a Pimm's Cup made with Sprite in a pinch.

Pimm's Cup

Makes 1 drink
Serve in a highball glass
7% ABV

1 ½ ounces Pimm's Cup No. 1
¼ ounce fresh lemon juice
4 ounces ginger ale
Cucumber peel and mint sprig or edible flowers for garnish

Combine Pimm's and lemon juice in a highball glass, add ice, and top with ginger ale. Garnish with cucumber peel and mint sprig or edible flowers.

I love this drink for a few reasons. One, it tastes delicious with just the right amount of bite from a mild green hot-sauce like Tabasco Green Pepper Sauce. Two, all the flavors enhance the tequila, which makes the drink feel more robust so that you don't miss the extra ounce of alcohol that most recipes would contain. Three, you can easily remove the tequila, making it alcohol-free, and it still tastes great.

Downward Tiger

Makes 1 drink
Serve in a cocktail glass
3% ABV

½ ounce tequila (optional)
1 ½ ounces lime juice
1 ½ ounces apple juice (fresh green apple juice, preferably juiced at home)
1 ounce honey syrup (see page 173)
½ ounce aquafaba (see page 49)
1 dash green chili hot sauce
6 drops salt tincture (see page 38)
Green apple slice for garnish (optional)

Combine ingredients with ice and shake vigorously. Strain the ice and then double shake without ice. Pour into a cocktail glass. Garnish with green apple slice.

A Comprehensive Guide to No- and Low-Alcohol Cocktails

Sometimes you just have to laugh at the origination myths of certain drinks. This one includes an erstwhile bartender using prosecco instead of gin, thus the Negroni "sbagliato," or mistaken Negroni. As a former bartender, I call bullshit. I've tossed dozens of drinks when I slipped and poured the wrong bottle; they were never this good. This drink is the product of careful consideration, and it shows in just how good it is.

Negroni Sbagliato

Makes 1 drink
Serve in a wine glass or double rocks glass
13% ABV

1 ounce Campari (or Lyre's Italian Orange; see page 32)
1 ounce sweet vermouth (or Lyre's Aperitif Rosso; see page 32)
1 ounce brut prosecco (or Thomson & Scott Noughty Alcohol-Free Sparkling Chardonnay; see page 36)
Thinly sliced orange peel for garnish

Combine all liquid ingredients in a glass, add ice, and stir. Garnish with thinly sliced orange peel.

A Comprehensive Guide to No- and Low-Alcohol Cocktails

There is the Bamboo, a cocktail with Sherry and dry vermouth, and then there's the Bamboo Shoot, my version, which adds sweet vermouth and three different kinds of bitters to turn the drink dark and rich and lovely.

Something to satisfy Manhattan drinkers who want to keep the booze down.

Bamboo Shoot

Makes 1 drink
Serve in a cocktail glass
12% ABV

1 ½ ounces dry amontillado Sherry
¾ ounce dry vermouth
¾ ounce sweet vermouth
1 dash celery bitters
1 dash aromatic bitters
1 dash orange bitters
Celery leaves for garnish

Combine all liquid ingredients in a mixing glass with ice and stir until chilled. Strain liquid into cocktail glass. Garnish with celery leaves.

Created as a twist on Satan's Whiskers (gin, orange curacao, sweet vermouth, dry vermouth, orange juice, orange bitters), this recipe drops the gin and increases the vermouth. It's an elegant drink and looks the part for those who don't want to give the impression of reducing their alcohol intake.

Straight Razor

Makes 1 drink
Serve in a cocktail glass
11% ABV

1 ounce sweet vermouth (or Lyre's Aperitif Rosso; see page 32)
1 ounce dry vermouth (or Lyre's Aperitif Dry; see page 32)
¼ ounce dry curacao (or Lyre's Orange Sec; see page 32)
1 ounce freshly squeezed orange juice
3 dashes orange bitters (preferably Fee Brothers West Indian Orange Bitters)
Orange peel for garnish

In a shaker, combine all liquid ingredients with ice and shake vigorously. Strain into cocktail glass and garnish with orange peel.

A Comprehensive Guide to No- and Low-Alcohol Cocktails

This is the most perfect cocktail that was ever made for me, by Hisashi Kishi of the Star Bar in Tokyo. A great cocktail bar in the Japanese-style, which is incredibly detailed and precise. It also marked the beginning of my love for Sherry, so it should come as no surprise how much I revere this cocktail.

Adonis

Makes 1 drink

Serve in a cocktail glass

13% ABV

2 ounces dry amontillado Sherry

1 ounce sweet vermouth

1 dash aromatic bitters

1 dash orange bitters

Orange peel for garnish

Combine all liquid ingredients in a mixing glass with ice and stir. Strain liquid into cocktail glass and garnish with orange peel.

A Comprehensive Guide to No- and Low-Alcohol Cocktails

This is my very dream of an aperitif. Of course, it follows that it must include vermouth. I believe vermouth should play a starring role in your low-alcohol cocktail repertoire. Here both sweet and dry vermouths make a showing with some non-alcoholic bubbly to keep the ABV down. Don't forget the salt!

<u>Add It Up</u>

Makes 1 drink
Serve in a cocktail glass
12% ABV

2 ounces sweet vermouth (or Lyre's Aperitif Rosso; see page 32)
1 ounce dry vermouth (or Lyre's Aperitif Dry; see page 32)
½ ounce non-alcoholic sparkling wine
6 drops salt tincture (see page 38)
Orange peel for garnish

Combine sweet and dry vermouths and salt tincture in a mixing glass with ice and stir. Strain liquid into cocktail glass. Float non-alcoholic sparkling wine on top and garnish with orange peel.

A Comprehensive Guide to No- and Low-Alcohol Cocktails

My absolute favorite drink of all time is the Dry Martini. I use equal parts dry gin and dry vermouth, a dash of orange bitters, stir until it's icy cold, and express a lemon peel on top before discarding the peel. This low-alcohol Martini version is the next best drink, if you want to lower the alcohol.

<u>Tinsy Ginsy</u>

Makes 1 drink
Serve in a cocktail glass
13% ABV

½ ounce London Dry gin (or Monday Gin; see page 33)
2 ¼ ounces dry vermouth (or Lyre's Aperitif Dry; see page 32)
1 dash orange bitters (Fee Brothers West Indian Orange Bitters preferred)
1 lemon peel

Combine all liquid ingredients in a mixing glass, add ice, and stir. Strain liquid into a chilled cocktail glass. Garnish with lemon peel.

A Comprehensive Guide to No- and Low-Alcohol Cocktails

There are few drinks that conjure summer as well as the Sherry Cobbler. Sure, the crushed ice and the fruit—hallmarks of the warmer months—have something to do with it, but it's also the Sherry. Oloroso Sherry, though it tastes a touch nutty with notes of dried fruits (apricots, apples, etc.), can also have flavors of red fruits, orange, and cherry, which come to the forefront in this drink.

Sherry Cobbler

Makes 1 drink
Serve in a highball or double rocks glass
13% ABV

2 ounces oloroso Sherry
½ ounce simple syrup (recipe, page 50)
2 thinly sliced orange wheels
Cherry and a mint sprig for garnish

In a shaker, combine Sherry, simple syrup, and 1 orange wheel, and shake vigorously. Pour into a highball, add crushed ice, and garnish with a skewered cherry, mint sprig, and the remaining orange wheel. Serve with a straw.

Low alcohol doesn't mean low fun. You can still make festive, fruity cocktails that can be enjoyed poolside (or barside, wishing you were poolside). With this one, my hope was that you'd forget whether it's low-proof or high-proof and just enjoy yourself.

Party Cruiser

Makes 1 drink
Serve in a cocktail glass
10% ABV

1 ½ ounces dry amontillado Sherry
¾ ounce pineapple juice
½ ounce orange curacao
1 dash fresh orange juice
½ ounce aquafaba (see page 49)
Cherry for garnish

In a shaker, combine ingredients with ice and shake vigorously. Remove ice and dry shake. Strain liquid into cocktail glass. Garnish with a cherry.

A Comprehensive Guide to No- and Low-Alcohol Cocktails

I always hear Loretta Lynn's refrain from her song "Portland, Oregon" with Jack White in my head whenever I make this drink: "Well, Portland, Oregon and sloe gin fizz/If that ain't love, then tell me what is, uh huh, uh huh...." Sloe gin is a liqueur made from gin, not surprisingly, and a relative of the plum: sloes. Good enough for the queen of country, good enough for me.

Sloe
Gin Fizz

Makes 1 drink
Serve in a highball glass
5% ABV

1 ½ ounces sloe gin
1 ounce fresh lemon juice
½ ounce simple syrup (recipe, page 50)
3 ounces soda water
Orange wheel and a cherry for garnish

In a shaker, combine gin, lemon juice, and simple syrup with ice and shake vigorously. Strain into highball glass, add fresh ice, and top with soda water. Garnish with orange wheel and cherry.

A Comprehensive Guide to No- and Low-Alcohol Cocktails

Sherry, Sherry, Sherry. Yes, I use a lot of Sherry in low-alcohol drinks. I also have two colada recipes. So, in many ways, this is the pinnacle of the book. This drink is incredibly tasty and still has wonderful complex flavors that keep it from being candy. Isn't that the goal for no- and low-alcoholic cocktails? Something better than the kiddie drinks we're usually served.

Sherry Colada

Makes 1 drink
Serve in a hurricane glass
5% ABV

2 ounces oloroso Sherry
1 ½ ounces pineapple juice
1 ½ ounces coconut cream
½ ounce fresh lime juice
6 drops salt tincture (see page 38)
Pineapple slice and frond for garnish

Combine all liquid ingredients in a blender with half a cup of ice and blend until smooth. Pour into hurricane glass and garnish with pineapple slice and frond.

A Comprehensive Guide to No- and Low-Alcohol Cocktails

There are complicated recipes for frosé and then there's this one. Scoop out some sorbet and add wine and syrup. This is the lazy person's frosé but it's just as good. Yes, the strawberry oleo saccharum adds a little extra time, but I've already admitted that I sometimes just cover strawberries with sugar and leave them overnight in the fridge, extracting the rich, red syrup at the bottom.

Frosé à la Minute

Makes 1 drink
Serve in a wine glass
2% ABV

4 ounces lemon sorbet
1 ounce rosé wine (or Non #1 Salted
Raspberry + Chamomile; see page 36)
½ ounce strawberry oleo saccharum (see
page 46)
Strawberry for garnish

Combine sorbet, wine, and strawberry oleo saccharum in a shaker and shake without ice. Pour into a wine glass and garnish with a strawberry.

A Comprehensive Guide to No- and Low-Alcohol Cocktails

The sangaree shares one thing with sangria—their names are both derived from the Latin word for blood—but that's where the similarities end. A sangaree has no fruit, save a dash of lemon juice, and also includes sugar and nutmeg. It can be made with just about any wine, sweet or dry. (This one is with red wine.) You just have to adjust the simple syrup to your taste.

Red Wine Sangaree

Makes 1 drink
Serve in double rocks glass
11% ABV

3 ounces syrah blend or other full-bodied dry red wine (or Jörg Geiger Inspiration 4.7, see page 36)
½ ounce simple syrup (recipe, page 50)
1 dash fresh lemon juice
Freshly grated nutmeg

Combine wine, simple syrup, and lemon juice in double rocks glass, add ice, and stir. Top with freshly grated nutmeg.

A Comprehensive Guide to No- and Low-Alcohol Cocktails

Some drinks are perfect just the way they are. They don't need to try to be something they are not, as is often the case when people try make a Michelada more like a Bloody Mary. Tomato juice is less important here—and in some cases absent altogether—than Maggi soy sauce and Tajín, a Mexican spice blend (although a little Clamato is a great addition). Sip and enjoy this savory concoction the way it was meant to be.

Michelada

Makes 1 drink
Serve in a pilsner glass
3% ABV

1 lime wedge
Tajín seasoning
6 ounces crisp lager (or Heineken 0.0; see page 33)
2 ounces Clamato
1 dash Maggi soy sauce
¼ ounce lime juice
1 dash hot pepper sauce

Rub a lime around the top rim and just on the outside of a pilsner glass and press the glass into a plate of Tajín seasoning. Combine the rest of the ingredients in the pilsner glass, add ice, and stir.

A Comprehensive Guide to No- and Low-Alcohol Cocktails

This is what you were meant to do with port. Don't get me wrong, port is good on its own, but it finds new purpose in a flip. Four simple ingredients create a sweet, rich dessert drink with an aromatic showering of nutmeg atop white foamy fluff, beckoning indulgence. Save this for a formal dinner or cozy night by the fire, or just don a smoking jacket and treat yourself.

Port Flip

Makes 1 drink
Serve in a wine or double rocks glass
9% ABV

2 ½ ounces tawny port
1 egg white
1 barspoon simple syrup (recipe, page 50)
Freshly grated nutmeg for garnish

In a shaker, combine ingredients with ice and shake vigorously. Strain liquid into wine glass. Garnish with grated nutmeg.

A Comprehensive Guide to No- and Low-Alcohol Cocktails

Mindful Wine is More Than Just Low-Alcohol

Wine is a great base for low-ABV cocktails. It has such a range of flavors, from the floral and citrus components of crisp white wines to the juicy fruit and spice flavors in rich red wines. Starting from the wine's profile, mixologists can be creative, drawing from historic drinks to making something no one has made before, but there's also an opportunity to do so much more than just make a great drink.

When I think about mindful drinking, I think of it as all encompassing. The choices we make have an impact on us, but they also have an impact on the world around us. That's not just in terms of how we feel, but in terms of social change. We can choose to support communities that benefit from our purchases.

The reason wine is unique, why it's more important in some ways than apples or textiles is, while it's an agricultural product, it's also preserved from nature. From an economic perspective, wine is a value added good. It has the power to create more dynamic markets in economically depressed areas—more jobs, higher streams of revenue, expanded educational opportunities. A mindful approach can support the environment and communities that can benefit from your purchases.

Rather than reaching for any old grocery store wine for your mindful wine cocktails, think about prioritizing wines from Georgia, Syria, Mexico, and Bolivia, where they increase the quality of life for that community. Better drinks, better lives. That's mindful drinking.

Maria Bastasch
Creator, Disco Mary

Chapter Seven
Putting It All Together

By now you should know that great cocktails don't have to be boozy or even have alcohol in them at all. You can have a cocktail, an adult sophisticated drink, on your own terms. It's a question of understanding what the underlying structure is for cocktails—intensity of flavor, texture, volume, and piquancy—and knowing what ingredients can get you there. I've laid out some ideas in this book and provided you with 60 recipes, but half the fun is making things up yourself.

Let's start by breaking cocktails down into four distinct categories: highball, aromatic, sour, and postprandial. While this doesn't cover every single cocktail ever created, it does provide a large umbrella for most cocktails. Out of these four categories, thousands of cocktails are made.

Highball

A highball is not technically a cocktail, but it is how we commonly refer to this typically two-ingredient drink today. A cocktail, traditionally, is more of an aromatic cocktail (see below), while a highball is with soda. This is your standard Vodka Soda, Gin and Tonic, Jack and Coke, but can also be creative as well. I always loved the variation on Rum and Coke from BlackTail, a now-closed Cuban-themed bar in New York City by Dead Rabbit owners Sean Muldoon and Jack McGarry, which effectively split the cola with Champagne, bitters, and Fernet Branca. In fact, I loved it so much it was the inspiration for my drink, Team Player.

To create a highball, you need to think about an intensely flavorful base and then add a soda or syrup and soda water. That base is somewhere around a third of the drink, generally speaking. An example is the Morrocan Mule I created, where a third of the drink is tea. In a drink like the Brunswick Cooler, on the other hand, the sum is greater than the parts. In the Brunswick Cooler there is two ounces of lemon juice but other ingredients, such as ginger, help support the intensity of the flavor.

Volume is another important factor in the highball. It's effectively a long drink, which means it should be served over ice in a tall glass. The volume of a highball is going to be greater than an aromatic cocktail (think Manhattan), about six ounces to four-and-a-half ounces when diluted. That has to be factored into the recipe.

A Comprehensive Guide to No- and Low-Alcohol Cocktails

Spirits, Sugar, Water, Bitters (Sometimes Acid)

Making beverages in your home does not have to be a daunting task. In fact, utilizing ingredients that you already have in your home is a challenge that you should take on. However, there are a few things that are key in ensuring the quality of your boozeless beverages:

1. Always use fresh juice. It is essential in making the most delicious drinks.

2. When making beverages, your base should always be spirits (or spirit substitute), sugar, water, and bitters, and occasionally acid.

Spirit, or Lack Thereof: With non-alcoholic beverages there are endless options for base substitutes. My personal favorite brand is Seedlip.

Sugar: Sugar balances your ingredients and accents flavor. Think about any time you've had tea and added a sweetener to it. Your flavors are enhanced. Honey, raw sugar, granulated cane sugar, and maple syrup are a great place to start.

Water: Water will dilute your beverage and make your drink cold and sometimes even hot. Water comes in the form of ice, soda, and is even present in your syrups. It is important to ensure that we are controlling the dilution and the temperature of our drinks.

Bitters: They are the salt and pepper of your beverage. Bitters are concentrated in flavor and season your drinks. If you are not consuming any alcohol, consider non-alcoholic bitters.

Acid: The addition of acid will turn your boozeless Old Fashioned variation into a classic sour. Make sure there is balance and intention behind how much acid you add to your drink. I love using vinegar, verjus, oranges, grapefruits, and even alternative acids, such as citric and tartaric acid.

3. Use classic cocktails as your inspiration when creating non-alcoholic drinks. Some of my favorite recipes include mimicking the Tom Collins and incorporating apple cider vinegar and orange juice as my acid instead of lemon juice. It adds a different flavor profile as well as complexity that the traditional lemonade with soda water does not have.

4. Have fun. Making cocktails should be fun and it is easy! Take all of these tips into consideration when making your spirit free beverages. The options are endless.

Lauren Paylor
Co-founder, Focus on Health

I'm going to do something controversial and lump spritzes in with highballs. Because they basically are. The main difference being you usually use a cordial or amaro as the base rather than, say, vodka, gin, or Bourbon. And they are sometimes split between soda and sparkling wine.

Aromatic

Aromatic cocktails are based on the first definition of an alcohol-based cocktail from 1806 and include spirits, sugar, water, bitters (not a plug for my previous book, but while we're at it . . .). An Old Fashioned is the prime example. The sugar is often replaced with vermouth or other liqueurs and cordials as with the Rob Roy (Scotch, sweet vermouth, orange bitters) or Negroni (gin, sweet vermouth, Campari).

The essence of an aromatic cocktail is that it's short and powerful. It's Napoleon without the complex. Unfortunately, this is the hardest drink to create with no- and low-alcohol ingredients. You need piquancy to really make it work. I suggest building aromatic cocktails around spicy, bold, and bitter flavors as I did with my Old Time Temperance Cocktail that uses hops and ginger.

Aromatic cocktails usually have about 2 ½ to 3 ounces of liquid before dilution, served up or on the rocks. While this drink is usually stirred in a mixing glass, you don't have to if it doesn't have a whole lot of texture to grab onto. Instead, build it on the glass and stir a lesser amount of strokes.

Of course, you can use non-alcoholic spirits. But they usually fall short of exact replicas, so don't be afraid to bolster with a spicy syrup, tannic tea, extra bitters, etc. I even reverse the ratios for some of the drinks with non-alcoholic vermouths and cordials, which are better analogs than most base non-alcoholic spirits. For example, I made a Martinez (gin, sweet vermouth, maraschino liqueur, orange bitters) variation using a non-alcoholic gin, sweet vermouth, and orange bitters but reversed the ratio of gin to sweet vermouth to 1:2.

Sour

This is the easier of the cocktail categories to make using no- and low-alcohol ingredients because the spirit is not always the focus. Take for instance a Bee's Knees, which is gin, lemon juice, and honey. The gin is an important factor but is practically smothered in honey-sweetened lemonade. Most sours have 1½ ounces of spirit and an ounce or so of juice and sweetener before dilution. However, that dilution can be significant.

With my Pinch Hitter, I came up with a base formula you can use for non-alcoholic sour cocktails:

> **2 ounces tart juice (lemon, lime, grapefruit, passionfruit, unsweetened cranberry, etc.)**
> **1 ounce ginger syrup (see page 41)**
> **1 teaspoon of apple cider vinegar**
> **½ ounce aquafaba (see page 49)**
> **6 drops salt tincture (see page 38)**

You may have to adjust the amount of juice or syrup, but this should give you a good place to start.

These are generally served up, but you can also transform this drink into a fizz or a Collins. A Fizz is with soda water but no ice, sometimes including eggs or egg whites, and the Collins is with soda and ice.

Postprandial

This is a catchall term I use for the rich, creamy, dessert-y cocktails, all the "cremes" really. Think Brandy Alexanders (Cognac, creme de cacao, and cream), Grasshoppers (white creme de menthe, creme de cacao, and cream), and Flips (spirits or wine with egg, sugar, and nutmeg).

With postprandial drinks, texture is everything. And that texture usually comes from dairy products or eggs (or dairy and egg substitutes). In that way, alcohol is the lesser part of the drink. I created my Maca Matcha Flip using oat milk, maca and matcha powders, and coconut oil, and it works quite well. To experiment, I recommend thinking of the whole volume as four to six ounces diluted, and playing with ingredients that work well in ice cream. Seriously. Green tea, coffee, chocolate all make great postprandial drinks. Add either cream, milk, or eggs (or dairy and egg substitutes) for the rest of the volume. Keep nutmeg handy.

There are the outliers, of course. Frosé is not really postprandial. It's Frosé. Beertails are another. But this is a good start to creating great no- and low-alcohol cocktails. The good news is that you don't necessarily have to spend a lot of money to play around at the base level. Ingredients like apple cider vinegar, lemons, and salt aren't particularly expensive. Obviously, you can rack it up from there buying non-alcoholic spirits, verjus, and fancy vinegars.

My overall advice is that creativity is overrated. Yes, a certain amount of creativity is necessary to experiment and try new things. But starting from known recipes and subbing this or that ingredient is a far more exacting strategy. Just like cooking, mixology is based on certain formulas that have been discovered, tested, and perfected over time. Even where those recipes are delivered in new and exciting presentations—a solid Pimm's Cup, or a Manhattan made into a balloon—they are derived from the classic formulations.

Afterword

In this book, I haven't once admonished you for drinking too much alcohol. Maybe that seems like the subtext: Don't drink so much, it's bad for you. But I've already admitted to my own failing in this regard. I drank too much. That doesn't mean it's a problem for you just because it was a problem for me. Or that drinking alcohol is something bad.

But you picked up this book. Unless you've always been a sober or moderate drinker, you made the choice to at least cut down on drinking alcohol, think about cutting down on drinking alcohol, or nudge a friend along in the same vein. Bartenders like myself shouldn't be the moral backbone of our society. We have our own issues, but we're the ones who have seen people at their absolute worst and best. We've seen you. Even when you think we didn't; alcohol has an amazing way of creating blinders to such observation and of making bar patrons think they're more charming than they really are.

And now I see you, too, but as a mindful drinker. I'm proud of you. No one else may realize that you have taken a brave step (not all of you, but some of you) and I want to say so. I see you, and I'm grateful to be part of your journey, whether you're tinkering around with no-and low-alcohol cocktails or this is deeply embedded in your lifestyle and I join your shelf with so many other great books on the subject. And I'd like to thank you, too, before I trail off and thank everyone else who helped me write this book. I really did write this book for you, but it's something that has greatly benefited me as well beyond its monetary value. We're on this journey together and, while that may be the only thing we agree on, it's something. And I pray it's something that in some small way connects us. Of all the travails that have beset us, from problem drinking to pandemics, the world is certainly not suffering from our ability to connect to one another, now is it?

I must start by thanking Caitlin Leffel who championed this idea from text message to text and, as before with my previous book, has been a wonderful collaborator throughout the process. And thank you to Rizzoli for entrusting me with a second book and to the various editors who touched the pages. I also want to thank Nole Garey for her beautiful pictures and Tony Lecy-Siewert for the design.

Many thanks go to Maria Bastasch for pushing me to write this book in the first place (an idea that germinated because of her), providing support during writing and researching, sharing her ideas along the way, and being my dream partner in life and work.

I owe a debt of gratitude to Julia Bainbridge for both her inspiration and words, and to the contributors: Ryan Chetiyawardan, Monique ten Kortenaar, Chris Marshall, Julia Momose, Lauren Paylor, and Camille Vidal, who are all innovators in the category. (Along with Tanya Cohn for some behind-the-scenes support.) Thank you, once again, to Bob Yule for being such a supporter, friend, and for looking over the text for me.

Thank you to David Wondrich and Anistatia Miller for providing context and discussion around the origin of the cocktail. And to Darcy O'Neil for his wonderful N.A. bitters recipe, and Victoria Vergason from The Hour in Alexandria, VA for lending me her beautiful glassware for pictures.

Thank you to the Columbia Room staff, especially Paul and Sherra, for helping to support the photo shoot and keeping watch over the house.

Thank you to Lauren, Abbey, and Lexie of Spiritless. And to all the brands and people pushing the category of no- and low-alcohol spirits, beer, wine, and cocktails. It's such an important and difficult role to be the early adopters—or "monkeys shot into space" as I like to call them—and to risk so much in pursuit of creating better choices.

Lastly, I want to thank Jesus Christ for walking me to the edge and showing me how steep the drop truly is from grace to Gehenna. Without that, I wouldn't have the courage to change the course of my life, removing alcohol from center and replacing it with his love.

Acknowledgments

First published in the United States of America in 2022 by
Rizzoli International Publications, Inc.
300 Park Avenue South
New York, NY 10010
www.rizzoliusa.com

Design & Art Direction: GCA

Publisher: Charles Miers
Editor: Caitlin Leffel
Production Manager: Colin Hough Trapp

Printed in China

2023 2024 2025 / 10 9 8 7 6 5 4 3

ISBN: 978-0-8478-7127-8
Library of Congress Control Number: 2021945358
Visit us online:
Facebook.com/RizzoliNewYork
Twitter: @Rizzoli_Books
Instagram.com/RizzoliBooks
Pinterest.com/RizzoliBooks
Youtube.com/user/RizzoliNY
Issuu.com/Rizzoli